David Earle Anderson
Plentywood – 2009

UPDIKE'S
VERSION

UPDIKE'S VERSION

Rewriting
The Scarlet Letter

James A. Schiff

University of Missouri Press
COLUMBIA AND LONDON

5 4 3 2 1   96 95 94 93 92

Library of Congress Cataloging-in-Publication Data

Schiff, James A., 1958–
    Updike's version : rewriting The scarlet letter / James A. Schiff.
      p.   cm.
    Includes bibliographical references and index.
    ISBN 0–8262–0871–1
    1. Updike, John—Criticism and interpretation. 2. Hawthorne,
Nathaniel, 1804–1864. Scarlet letter. 3. Hawthorne, Nathaniel,
1804–1864—Influence. 4. Influence (Literary, artistic, etc.)
5. Updike, John—Knowledge—Literature. I. Title.
PS3571.P4Z874   1992
813'.54—dc20   92–26726
                                             CIP

♾™ This paper meets the requirements of the
American National Standard for Permanence of Paper
for Printed Library Materials, Z39.48, 1984.

Designer: Elizabeth Fett
Typesetter: Connell-Zeko Type & Graphics
Printer and Binder: Thomson-Shore, Inc.
Typeface: California

FOR
BETH AND WALKER,
ADELE AND BOB

CONTENTS

ACKNOWLEDGMENTS

As a student at Duke University in the early 1980s I was fortunate enough to take two courses in creative writing with Reynolds Price. Through Mr. Price, whose tower office floated like a holy sanctum over the campus, I discovered that literature does indeed *matter*, and that a career in literature is possible. For that I thank him, and also for his final advice: "Read Updike," he said. And I have.

I would like to thank those friends, colleagues, and professors who have read earlier drafts of the manuscript and made acute suggestions: David Hicks, James Seitz, David DeVries, Ronald Kasdorf, Frederick Karl, Josephine Hendin. My greatest debt though is to James W. Tuttleton, whose support, advice, and encouragement have been instrumental in seeing this project grow from an idea into a tangible product.

I would also like to thank my parents, for their assistance, both financial and emotional, and for their undying confidence; Beth, who has had to put up with me on a daily basis (no easy task), and who has provided more support and love than I have deserved; and Walker, who arrived just in time to teach me that there are many more important things in the world than Dad's book.

I am indebted to Alfred A. Knopf, Inc., and to André Deutsch, Ltd., for their permission to quote from the following copyrighted Updike works: *Assorted Prose* (1965), *A Month of Sundays* (1975), *Picked-Up Pieces* (1976), *Hugging the Shore* (1983), *Roger's Version* (1986), *S.* (1988), and *Odd Jobs* (1991). I also wish to thank the editors of *Studies in American Fiction* and *South Atlantic Review* for their permission to use material from my published essays. Portions of the Introduction and Chapters 1, 2, and 3 were originally published in *Studies in American Fiction* 20.1 (1992), and portions of Chapter 2 first appeared in *South Atlantic Review* 57.4 (1992). And finally, I wish to thank Beverly Jarrett, for her confidence in my work, and John Updike, for permission to quote from our correspondence. Mr. Updike's prompt and gracious replies have provided assistance and inspiration.

ABBREVIATIONS

The following abbreviations appear parenthetically throughout the text to identify frequently cited works:

Nathaniel Hawthorne

BR   *The Blithedale Romance and Fanshawe.* Volume 3 of *The Centenary Edition of the Works of Nathaniel Hawthorne.* William Charvat, Roy Harvey Pearce, and Claude M. Simpson, general editors. Columbus: Ohio State University Press, 1971.

SL   *The Scarlet Letter.* Volume 1 of *The Centenary Edition of the Works of Nathaniel Hawthorne.* William Charvat, Roy Harvey Pearce, and Claude M. Simpson, general editors. Columbus: Ohio State University Press, 1962.

John Updike

MS   *A Month of Sundays.* New York: Knopf, 1975.

RV   *Roger's Version.* New York: Knopf, 1986.

UPDIKE'S VERSION

INTRODUCTION
The Scarlet Letter as Myth

Though many readers are aware of how John Updike has chronicled America of the 1950s, 1960s, 1970s, and 1980s in his "Rabbit tetralogy," few have paid close attention to his other multivolume work concerning America (and a canonical American text), namely, the "*Scarlet Letter* trilogy." In 1975 Updike published *A Month of Sundays*, a novel in diary form in which a spiritually tormented and adulterous minister from Massachusetts is ordered to an Arizona motel for ministers-gone-astray; there he is urged to wrestle with his perverse soul and rub out his "stain." Updike later referred to that novel as "Dimmesdale's version" of *The Scarlet Letter.*[1] In 1986 Updike published *Roger's Version*, an unreliable first-person narrative in which a Harvard professor, a crusty old doctor of divinity named Roger, manipulates and feeds upon the life of a youthful, pious computer-science graduate student named Dale. Most recently, in 1988 Updike published the epistolary novel S., in which an angry North Shore housewife, with a strong predilection for vitamin A, rebels against her Puritan heritage and patriarchal society by traveling to a desert ashram in Arizona. In these three novels, each told from the perspective of a contemporary version of one of Hawthorne's three protagonists in *The Scarlet Letter*—Arthur Dimmesdale, Roger Chillingworth, and Hester Prynne—Updike has expanded, up-

---

1. Updike states that the conflict between matter and spirit is central in Hawthorne's work, and "where the two incompatible realms of Hawthorne's universe impinge, something leaks through; there is a *stain.* . . . The stain, this sinister spillage from another world, can take the form of poison, of a potion . . . of overinsistent symbols like the scarlet letter" ("Hawthorne's Creed," 77); for Updike's reference to *A Month of Sundays* as "Dimmesdale's version," see "A 'Special Message' for the Franklin Library's First Edition Society Printing of *Roger's Version* (1986)," 858. Updike also speaks of how his trilogy retells *The Scarlet Letter* in "Unsolicited Thoughts on S. (1988)."

1

dated, satirized, and rewritten Hawthorne's text, creating his own *Scarlet Letter* trilogy.

That such a bold and intriguing project should go largely unexplored by the critical community is surprising. Though these novels, with the notable exception of *Roger's Version*, may appear to be lighter fare and less substantial than the best of Updike (the Rabbit novels, *The Centaur, The Coup*), initial readings are deceiving, particularly since these novels are trickier and more multilayered than the more conventionally realistic Rabbit tetralogy. *Roger's Version*, to my mind, is one of the most exceptional volumes to date in Updike's oeuvre, and *A Month of Sundays* and *S.* deserve far closer scrutiny than they have received from all but a few critics.[2] In fact, all three novels reveal a more postmodern Updike, one who experiments with alternative narrative modes, such as the diary and the epistolary novel, in creating texts that are highly self-reflexive and cleverly intertextual. In addition, the trilogy discloses an increasingly more erudite Updike, who has mastered and integrated into his novels a wealth of difficult information from such disciplines as computer science, particle physics, evolution theory, cosmology, ecclesiology, early-Christian heresy, Hinduism, and Buddhism. However, no matter what value a reader may assign to the novels of Updike's trilogy, the project remains significant because any reconsideration of a canonical text by a major literary figure such as Updike warrants attention, particularly in light of so much contemporary interest in intertextuality.

To understand the critical response to such a recently completed project as Updike's trilogy, one must examine both book reviews and scholarly articles. Typically, reviewers of these three Updike novels have been aware of the *Scarlet Letter* parallels and have commented upon the comic allusions; however, as one re-

---

2. *S.* has yet to receive a close critical reading, and there exist few adequate and detailed analyses of *A Month of Sundays*. An exception to the norm, Samuel Chase Coale finds that *A Month of Sundays* "achieves the vision that *Couples* muddled, that *Rabbit, Run* avoided," and he refers to it as Updike's triumph as a romancer (*In Hawthorne's Shadow: American Romance from Melville to Mailer*, 139–46). See also John T. Matthews, "The Word as Scandal: Updike's *A Month of Sundays*"; Gary Waller, "Stylus Dei or the Open-Endedness of Debate? Success and Failure in *A Month of Sundays*"; and George W. Hunt, S.J., *John Updike and the Three Great Secret Things: Sex, Religion, and Art*, 181–207.

viewer puts it, "what purpose these references serve is not so clear," and "it remains debatable whether the failure" to notice Updike's "somewhat cryptic references to Nathaniel Hawthorne's *Scarlet Letter*" makes much difference. Another reviewer refers to Updike's "direct exploitation" of Hawthorne's novel as "thin and half-hearted," and a third reviewer, upon bashing the final volume of the trilogy, *S.*, remarks: "I look forward, though, to the third volume of the trilogy, which will feature a contemporary version of Arthur Dimmesdale"; little did she realize that that book had been published thirteen years prior.[3] My point, perhaps less than astonishing, is that reviewers have not exercised much care in following the dialogue between Updike and Hawthorne, and that a climate has been created that acknowledges the intertextual comedy but fails to attribute any significance to it.

As expected, scholarly articles and books have scrutinized more carefully the relationship between Updike and Hawthorne. However, most scholars have yet to acknowledge the depth and extent of Hawthorne's significance, particularly as it figures in Updike's most Hawthornesque work, his *Scarlet Letter* trilogy. The two studies that address the relationship at greatest length and deal with how Hawthorne's influence is felt in such Updike novels as *Couples, A Month of Sundays*, and *Rabbit, Run* are Samuel Chase Coale's *In Hawthorne's Shadow* (1985) and Donald J. Greiner's *Adultery in the American Novel: Updike, James, and Hawthorne* (1985). Both are valuable and significant in establishing a foundation for understanding this relationship; Coale links the two writers through the dualism of Manichaeanism, and Greiner links them through their responses to and their depiction of adultery. However, both of these studies appeared before the second and third volumes of Updike's trilogy; in other words, they appeared before the extent of Updike's interest in Hawthorne was known.

---

3. Christopher Lehmann-Haupt, "In John Updike's Latest, The Woman Called *S.*"; Richard Gilman, "The Witches of Updike," 40; Alison Lurie, "The Woman Who Rode Away," 4. I should append that there have indeed been some insightful reviews. For *A Month of Sundays*, see Rosemary Dinnage, "Lusting for God"; and George Steiner, "Scarlet Letters." For *Roger's Version*, see Richard Eder, "Roger's Version"; David Lodge, "Chasing after God and Sex"; Ann-Janine Morey, "Updike's Sexual Language for God"; and Nicholas Spice, "Underparts." For *S.*, see John Lanchester, "Be a Lamp unto Yourself."

Since 1988 several notable articles have appeared discussing the dialogue between Hawthorne and Updike as seen in a single volume of the trilogy, namely *Roger's Version:* John N. Duvall, "The Pleasure of Textual/Sexual Wrestling: Pornography and Heresy in *Roger's Version*"; James A. Schiff, "Updike's *Roger's Version:* Re-Visualizing *The Scarlet Letter*"; and Raymond Wilson III, "*Roger's Version:* Updike's Negative-Solid Model of *The Scarlet Letter.*" Only two articles, however, have appeared examining the entire trilogy: Donald J. Greiner, "Body and Soul: John Updike and *The Scarlet Letter*"; and James A. Schiff, "Updike's *Scarlet Letter* Trilogy: Recasting an American Myth." These articles do much to assist in understanding the intertextual dialogue; however, Updike's project is far more complex than has yet been acknowledged, and so much of the dialogue remains unexplored and unaccounted for—thus, the reason for this study.

Some readers, no doubt, may be surprised by Updike's project: Why explicitly rewrite a story that has already been told so successfully? And why Hawthorne? In answer to the former, one must consider how often Updike has relied upon the work of previous writers. His first novel, *The Poorhouse Fair* (1958), was a futuristic retelling of the story of St. Stephen. *Rabbit, Run* (1960) sprang from Jack Kerouac's *On the Road*, Arthurian grail legend, and Peter Rabbit. *The Centaur* (1963) updated and interlaced a variety of Greek myths—so many, in fact, that Updike, at his wife's suggestion, compiled a mythological index as an appendix. And *Couples* (1968) relied greatly upon the legends of Tristan and Iseult, Lot in Sodom, Don Juan, and the Fall from Eden. The mythic mode, in which a writer appropriates and retells an earlier story or tale that has achieved mythic dimensions, has long been salient in Updike's fiction, though critics have failed to recognize its importance except in *The Centaur.* Updike himself has spoken of how, in *The Centaur,* he not only retold earlier myths but also revealed how certain myths persist in contemporary culture: "The natural events in my book are meant to be a kind of mask for the myth."[4] Beneath the guise of contemporary, quotidian small-town

---

4. "One Big Interview," 499; in this anthology of interviews, Updike speaks at some length about the mythic mode and about the sources of his fiction.

life, Updike reveals a mythic foundation that operates as "a counterpoint of ideality to the drab real level" and lends a heroic stature to rather ordinary small-town events. In addition, the mythic mode for Updike provides "an excuse for a number of jokes," and it expresses his "sensation that the people we meet are *guises*, do conceal something mythic, perhaps prototypes or longings in our minds."[5]

In answer to the latter question, "Why Hawthorne?" one might wonder why Updike did not turn, in a Bloomian sense of "anxiety of influence," to writers who have exercised a greater influence over him, such as Joyce, Nabokov, Proust, and Henry Green, or even to other American writers who have captured his attention, such as Melville, Howells, James, Hemingway, Salinger, and John O'Hara. Updike no doubt could have recast Melville's Ahab and Ishmael as investment bankers on Wall Street, heroically attempting the takeover of a major oil conglomerate known respectfully as the Great White Corporation. Yet Updike chose Hawthorne and *The Scarlet Letter.* Why? As the contemporary American chronicler of adultery, Updike provides a reasonable explanation: "[*The Scarlet Letter*] is our *Anna Karenina* and *Madame Bovary.* It is our contribution to the novel of adultery." The author of *Couples* has never failed to express his interest in, and perhaps even obsession with, what Tony Tanner calls the "unstable triangularity of adultery." And it is natural that Updike should be drawn to reexamine and even rewrite what he himself calls "the one classic from the lusty youth of American literature that deals with society in its actual heterosexual weave." Though Tanner contends that in contemporary literature "adultery . . . no longer signifies" because of a "slackening of tension between passion and society," critics such as Barbara Leckie and John Neary point to how the adulterous impulse in Updike's characters continues to offer transcendence and "the dim promise of the untouched, the immediate, even the sacred."[6]

5. Updike, Interview with Charles Thomas Samuels, 442.
6. For Updike's answer to the question, "Why Hawthorne?" see Appendix; Updike, Interview with Mervyn Rothstein, "In S., Updike Tries the Woman's Viewpoint"; Tanner, *Adultery in the Novel: Contract and Transgression*, 12; Updike, "A 'Special Message' [*Roger's Version*]," 858; Tanner, *Adultery in the Novel*, 89; Leckie, "'The Adulterous Society': John Updike's *Marry Me*," 64; Neary, *Something*

In addition to adultery, Updike discovered in Hawthorne other themes and conflicts inherent in his own writing: the conflict between matter and spirit, a fascination with community and communal experiments, the anxiety and fear of moral damnation, the interrelationship between sex and religion, and the use of ambivalent symbolism. The link between the two writers is strengthened by the fact that both have lived most of their lives on approximately the same patch of ground near Boston—Hawthorne in Salem and Concord, and Updike in Ipswich, Cambridge, Georgetown, and Beverly Farms. Hawthorne has become more than just a literary antecedent for Updike; he is a figure embedded in the history and myth of Updike's chosen community, a writer whose town Updike must pass every time he goes to and from Boston.[7]

Yet in appropriating Hawthorne's text, Updike ostensibly was driven by more than just similarities between his work and that of Hawthorne; he must have hoped to gain some benefit. Though enormously successful in both critical and popular circles, Updike has been rather viciously attacked by a small group of critics for lacking depth, for capturing "only the outside of things, the shell of the corporate experience we all have in being twentieth-century Americans." These critics tend to view him as a writer who is all style and little content: "Updike, out of kindness or acedia, has very little to say. And no one writing in America says it better."[8] In light of Updike's often eager responsiveness to address his critics, it seems likely, as Denis Donoghue suggests, that by rewriting *The Scarlet Letter* Updike was expressing "his middle-aged determination to give his art a metaphysical darkening."[9] And as witnessed

and Nothingness: The Fiction of John Updike and John Fowles, 177.

7. When traveling to Boston by rail, Updike actually passes underneath Salem. As he writes in his essay "A Short and Happy Ride," "The train takes a dark plunge into the earth beneath Salem. . . . Perhaps the ominous darkness fittingly memorializes Hawthorne" (62).

8. Richard H. Rupp, "John Updike: Style in Search of a Center," 17; D. Keith Mano, "Doughy Middleness," 76. For other critical attacks on Updike, see John W. Aldridge, *Time to Murder and Create: The Contemporary Novel in Crisis;* Norman Podhoretz, *Doings and Undoings;* and Frederick Crews, "Mr. Updike's Planet."

9. "'I Have Preened, I Have Lived,'" 7. As for his responsiveness to his critics, Updike, in regard to his portrayal of women, states in the Rothstein interview, "Woman's Viewpoint": "But knowing that there is this reservation out in some

in recent novels—*The Witches of Eastwick* (1984), *Roger's Version* (1986), and *Rabbit at Rest* (1990)—there is now a darker resonance, a more sustained reflection upon death and solitude, and a growing interest in voyeurism and vicariously experienced life.

Updike becomes the latest apprentice in what Richard H. Brodhead refers to as "The School of Hawthorne." According to Brodhead, Hawthorne, unlike Whitman or Emerson, was so "uncommunicative" and gave such little guidance to his followers that they "have been free to put him to any purpose they have required." Writers from Melville, James, and Howells to the present have been able to reinvent Hawthorne so as to suit their own personal needs, creating or aligning themselves with "the Hawthorne tradition" and appropriating the authority and success that are conferred by such a tradition. In turning to Hawthorne, Updike carves out an emotional stance for himself that expresses a "mixture of devotion . . . and aggression" toward his predecessor. Through his intertextual echoings, Updike works to maintain and confirm a connection with the past, offering homage to an earlier writer and text. The author of a series of essays on writers whom he refers to as "American Masters" (Emerson, Franklin, Hawthorne, Howells, Melville, and Whitman), Updike has long expressed his awareness and reverence for such writers and for the hierarchy that confirms such a status.[10] In his utilization of Hawthorne, Updike endeavors to absorb some degree of his predecessor's genius and align himself as another New England writer within a tradition of American masters, in hopes no doubt that his work at some point will be pondered in relation to Hawthorne's. Yet that is only part of the picture. Updike also parodies and deromanticizes Hawthorne's text, calling into question its authority and moral stance. With his clinical frankness and post-Freudian desire to verbalize, Updike

---

quarters about my portraits of women, I'm constantly trying to improve them. . . . *The Witches of Eastwick* . . . was one attempt to make things right with my, what shall we call them, feminist detractors, and [S.] is another" ("Woman's Viewpoint"). The warning, of course, is to keep in mind Updike's tendency toward irony, particularly since these two novels have most angered feminist critics.

10. Brodhead, *The School of Hawthorne*, 15–16; Heidi Ziegler, "Love's Labours Won: The Erotics of Contemporary Parody," 60; Updike, "Emersonianism," "Many Bens," "Hawthorne's Creed," "Howells as Anti-Novelist," "Melville's Withdrawal," and "Whitman's Egotheism."

rejects the warfare between body and soul, which is so central to Hawthorne, and he satirizes Hawthorne's protagonists for their fragility, prudishness, and self-deception. Updike's stance toward Hawthorne is complex; he pays homage to the past "master" and yet questions and satirizes the master's moral tenets.

In attempting to transform Hawthorne's text, Updike is seeking to alter an American myth. Explaining his project, Updike states that "*The Scarlet Letter* is not merely a piece of fiction, it is a myth by now, and it was an updating of the myth, the triangle as redefined by D. H. Lawrence, that interested me." Though one must be careful in following critical paths set down by an author, Updike's words are of great utility. By referring to Hawthorne's novel as a "myth," Updike appears to use the term not primarily in the sense of indicating a primitive pattern of behavior, as the term might be used to suggest by Mircea Eliade, Joseph Campbell, Northrop Frye, C. G. Jung, and others, but more specifically as a story or a pattern of behavior "linked with a particular culture and dealing with named characters and locations" as generated in a work of literature.[11] In his famous essay on Denis de Rougemont, Updike, speaking playfully about national characters and myths, offers the possibility that a myth "represents the *bad conscience* of its nation, the defect of the national psyche magnified and propelled forward into a logical doom," and he remarks how Tristan and Don Juan, Faust and Don Quixote may be interpreted as "the national myths of, respectively, France, Italy, Germany, and Spain." Accordingly, what text better answers to the "bad conscience" of the American psyche and its "logical doom" than *The Scarlet Letter*? And the case for Hawthorne's novel as America's national myth is further strengthened by René Wellek and Austin Warren's definition of a myth as "the explanation a society offers its young of why the world is and why we do as we do."[12] As witnessed in high-school English curricula across the nation, Hawthorne's novel of adulterous love and communal oppression, per-

---

11. Updike, Letter to the author, January 26, 1989; John J. White, *Mythology in the Modern Novel*, 38.

12. Updike, "More Love in the Western World," 295; William Righter quoting Wellek and Warren, *Myth and Literature*, 5.

haps more than any other text, is what America offers its young, both as literature and as history.

According to Eric Gould, "myths apparently derive their universal significance from the way in which they try to reconstitute an original event."[13] That event in *The Scarlet Letter* is of course the formation of America as the New Eden, a "City upon a Hill," enacted by a covenant between God and His chosen people. Hawthorne's novel fictively captures the genesis of a nation and attempts to reconstruct the incipient moral dilemmas and conflicts that would later evolve into Hawthorne's own Victorian culture. *The Scarlet Letter* limns an America threatened by Eros, marred by deception and hypocrisy, wracked with guilt, obsessed with maintaining pure appearances, and inclined to point accusing fingers. And if we were to isolate upon a single scene in *The Scarlet Letter* and interpret it as the representative "original event," one need look no further than to what is perhaps the primal scene in American literature: Hester exposed on the scaffold before the oppressive eyes of the community (one could also argue that the "original event" is the absent scene, that of coitus between Hester and Dimmesdale). Hester's public exposure and chastisement by her fellow citizens for her sexual misconduct is archetypal in American culture, and variations upon the scene have been replayed many times over in American history by both men and women, most recently with the ministerial sex scandals involving Jimmy Swaggart and Jim Bakker, and the political sex scandals with Gary Hart and Donna Rice, Clarence Thomas and Anita Hill.

At its core a myth expresses, as de Rougemont points out, "the *rules of conduct* of a given social or religious group," and it exposes how the individuals of that historical group relate to one another. In Hawthorne's text, characters remain largely isolated from one another, residing in separate "spheres" and rarely touching. Human contact, in particular coitus between Hester and Dimmesdale, is a legal and moral violation. According to Updike, "Hawthorne's instinctive tenet [is] that matter and spirit are inevitably at war," and in the course of this battle, "matter verges upon being evil;

13. *Mythical Intentions in Modern Literature*, 6.

virtue, upon being insubstantial."[14] Hawthorne's characters are literally divided between public and private self, interior and exterior world, body and soul. And as seen in Dimmesdale's dramatic death upon the scaffold, the soul, apparently with Hawthorne's approval, is victorious over the transgressions of the body. In his trilogy, Updike endeavors to transform the *Scarlet Letter* myth by affirming corporeal impulse and thus reconciling body and soul.

As far as the reference to Lawrence, Updike's trilogy appropriates and builds upon two concepts outlined in Lawrence's *Studies in Classic American Literature:* Hawthorne's duplicity and the American quest for renewal. According to Lawrence, the primary impulse in Hawthorne is toward subversion and deception: "That blue-eyed darling Nathaniel knew disagreeable things in his inner soul. He was careful to send them out in disguise." In recasting Hester, Dimmesdale, and Chillingworth, Updike, like Lawrence before him, compels the reader to reexamine the nature of Hawthorne's characters, particularly in regard to what has been repressed or disguised. For instance, Hester, who many readers find to be stoic and saintly, is reshaped by Lawrence as a "gentle devil" who desires to revenge herself upon the male species. A caveat, however, is necessary here in regard to gender issues. Feminist critics in particular have voiced strong opposition to Lawrence's understanding of male-female relationships, and they have argued, often convincingly, that aspects of his writing promote sexual hostility and violence. Within some parts of the critical community, Lawrence has come to wear the letter *M* as his badge of shame, signifying *Misogynist.* In Hawthorne studies, however, Lawrence's reading of *The Scarlet Letter* continues for many (myself included) to be significant and largely persuasive. In a recent essay, Michael Davitt Bell, a leading Hawthorne scholar, takes up Lawrence's argument, contending, like Lawrence, that the primary impulse in Hawthorne is toward subversion and deception. Bell remarks that "in the past twenty years or so, we have become more sensitive to this hidden quality in Hawthorne's fiction," and

14. De Rougemont, *Love in the Western World,* 18; Updike, "Hawthorne's Creed," 77.

he speaks of Lawrence as "the fountainhead of this view."[15] Though Lawrence may be an offensive and unfavorable presence to some readers, his influence remains significant.

In addition, Lawrence speaks of the self's ability for "shedding skins," a term that Updike appropriates in *S.* Lawrence explains the founding of America as arising not from a desire by the "Pilgrim Fathers" for freedom, but as a desire "largely to get *away*. . . . To get away from everything they are and have been." The objective was to slough off the old European skin and grow a new American one. Updike's characters, in an America of the 1970s and 1980s, find themselves in a rather similar situation, though it is no longer a European skin that must be sloughed off. Bored and oppressed by their own predictable lives and by a repressive middle-class Protestantism (handed down from Hawthorne's characters), Updike's characters are in need of passionate experience, what de Rougemont refers to as a "transfiguring force."[16] And so they follow the same spirit of quest that once lured Hawthorne's characters across the Atlantic. In his *Scarlet Letter* novels—*A Month of Sundays, Roger's Version,* and *S.*—Updike recasts Hawthorne's three "divided" protagonists and demonstrates how the "mythic" American situation persists: that of individuals struggling within themselves and against their communities in an effort to shake off the past and reinvent the world.

If, like Updike, we are to treat Hawthorne's novel as a myth, we must address ourselves to the specific critical questions and problems that arise when a contemporary novelist attempts to retell an earlier story that has achieved mythic significance. Each of Updike's three novels is an example of what John J. White refers to as the "mythological novel," a work of fiction that, rather than offering a new myth, "presents a modern situation and refers the reader to a familiar analogy." In his essay "*Ulysses*, Order, and Myth" (1923), T. S. Eliot explains Joyce's reliance on the *Odyssey* in what has become the archetypal mythological novel, *Ulysses*:

15. Lawrence, *Studies*, 89; Bell, "Arts of Deception: Hawthorne, 'Romance,' and *The Scarlet Letter*," 29, 54.
16. Lawrence, *Studies*, 9; de Rougemont, *Love*, 16.

In using the myth, in manipulating a continuous parallel between contemporaneity and antiquity, Mr. Joyce is pursuing a method which others must pursue after him. They will not be imitators, any more than the scientist who uses the discoveries of an Einstein in pursuing his own, independent, further investigations. It is simply a way of controlling, of ordering, of giving a shape and a significance to the immense panorama of futility and anarchy which is contemporary history. . . . Instead of narrative method, we may now use the mythical method.

Updike himself has expressed mild bewilderment as to precisely what Eliot meant: "Does he mean that we are ourselves so depleted of psychic energy, of spiritual and primitive force, that we can do little but retell old stories?" Although Updike appears to treat the mythical method as an attractive alternative rather than as a mandate, what survives from Eliot's essay is the insistence that myth offers a structure, a form. William Righter speaks of the myth as a mannequin in a shop window upon which all sorts of changing displays may be exhibited.[17] The myth thus provides an order, a body, a form from which imaginative opportunities present themselves. However, as we shall see in Updike's trilogy, the myth operates as more than just a static scaffold; rather there is a more protean notion of structure and correspondence between *The Scarlet Letter* and Updike's novels.

In this century, and particularly since Joyce, a number of novels and long poems have retold earlier myths; as White points out, the mythical method is very much "in the air." Writers such as Faulkner, Lawrence, Yeats, Mann, Anthony Burgess, Bernard Malamud, John Barth, Jean Rhys, Max Frisch, Nikos Kazantzakis, Derek Walcott, Robert Coover, Thomas Berger, Jane Smiley, and Updike himself (in *The Centaur,* most conspicuously) have employed what we shall call the *mythical method.* And though their reasons for doing so may vary, they share a common aim: to present to the reader an interesting contemporary story, and at the same time to make him "feel [as if] the chosen analogy has enriched his understanding of the primary material." Pure "slavish imitation" would of course be "devoid of surprise and lacking in life,"

17. White, *Mythology,* 23; Eliot, *"Ulysses,* Order, and Myth," 177–78; Updike, Interview with Charles Thomas Samuels, 443; Righter, *Myth,* 33.

and so in his recasting, the contemporary writer must change his attitude, shift the emphasis, and focus upon different aspects of the earlier story. The myth, as John B. Vickery suggests, is a challenge for a writer because "it dares him to tell the same story differently, conveying his own attitude toward it and exemplifying his own solution to the problems of technique inherent in the tale."[18]

Reading a novel that retells a myth presents unique problems. Although all novels intrinsically create expectations for the reader, the mythological novel is unique in creating quite specific expectations. For instance, in *A Month of Sundays*, the reader anticipates that Thomas Marshfield, the Dimmesdale figure, will have a romantic affair with the desert motel manageress, Ms. Prynne, Updike's Hester figure. Yet Ms. Prynne, "a large lady, undeformed but unattractive," is neither beautiful nor appealing like her literary ancestor, and in addition, she appears most impenetrable and unyielding (*MS*, 6). Updike's novel works against expectations as the reader wonders why Marshfield should desire to seduce this very different Ms. Prynne. And while awaiting the outcome, the reader is forced to reexamine the relationship between the mythic or prefigurative characters, Dimmesdale and Hester, and search for alternative explanations as to why the attraction exists.[19] In this particular novel, Updike seems more interested in the Hester figure as a person of authority. Maintaining control over the desert community, Updike's Ms. Prynne is a keeper of men, a matronly manageress who assumes power over weakened and fallen religious men. Updike's novel forces the reader to reexamine the relationship between Hawthorne's Hester and Dimmesdale in terms of the role of power, control, and authority.

In addition, characters in a mythological novel possess a multidimensional degree of self. For instance, Sarah Worth of *S.* is not just Sarah Worth; she is also Hester Prynne, and however she functions as a character is a comment upon Hester. Whether or not she has sexual relations with the Indian guru is a central element in

18. White, *Mythology*, 30, 90–91, 108, 112; Vickery, *Myths and Texts: Strategies of Incorporation and Displacement*, 28.

19. Though the term *prefiguration* commonly carries with it the suggestion of prophecy in discussions of typology, when used in the secular sense it refers analogically to that which came before.

the plot of *S.*, yet it is also significant in regard to *The Scarlet Letter*, since coitus between Sarah and the guru offers a comment upon coitus between Hester and Dimmesdale. An essential caveat, however, and to some degree a retraction, is to remember that although Sarah is Hester, she is *not quite* Hester. Differences persist, particularly in regard to how each operates within a distinctive environment and text. In following the movements of Sarah, the reader sees a multidimensional self composed of Sarah Worth, Hester Prynne, and the point of intersection between the two.

As already noted, there is not always a "persistent, one-to-one relationship" between the prefigurative myth and the mythological novel; prefigurations often occur in "more complex patterns and in greater numbers." This sense of "distortion" is best discussed by utilizing two terms initially applied to patterns of distortion found in dreams: *fragmentation* and *condensation*. Fragmentation occurs when a single mythical character is fragmented into or refracted across a number of contemporary characters, leading those contemporary characters into playing varying aspects of a single mythic type.[20] An example of fragmentation occurs in *Roger's Version*, in which both Esther Lambert and Verna Ekelof play the role of Hester. Strong-willed and adamant, both women find themselves in triangular relationships with the Dimmesdale and Chillingworth figures in the novel. Whereas Esther, however, plays a middle-class housewife variety of Hester, Verna plays a more unpolished and desperate version of Hawthorne's heroine.

A similar form of distortion known as condensation refers to a situation in which more than one prefiguration is related to a single contemporary character or event; in other words, several prefigurative characters have been condensed into one contemporary character. In *A Month of Sundays*, Marshfield is the Dimmesdale figure, yet at the beginning he appears more like Hester: "I felt, being served this morning, dealt with reverentially, or dreadfully, as if in avoidance of contamination" (*MS*, 5). And later, when he assumes the role of the voyeur by spying upon his young curate,

20. White, *Mythology*, 193, 191–240. In utilizing the terms fragmentation and condensation, White points out that he does not desire to create a parallel between mythological novels and dreams.

Ned Bork, and his organist/lover, Alicia Crick, he becomes a Chillingworth figure. Condensation and fragmentation occur in all three of Updike's novels, providing for new combinations and possibilities, which may alter and enhance our understanding of the underlying mythic triangle. In addition, these modes of distortion suggest that in an adulterous triangle the roles are variable and protean, and that each character may come to play, at least temporarily, the roles of the other two characters. Finally, as White suggests, the "maze of fragmented and condensed prefigurations . . . suits an age of uncertain values and indeterminate standards of guilt and innocence," certainly the "opposite function" to those who suggest that the contemporary novel uses myth in order to "simplify the chaos of the modern world."[21]

Of course a common feature found in mythological novels, as evident from Sarah Worth's predilection for vitamin A and Thomas Marshfield's pajama-clad midnight vigil, is parody and comedy. Although the mythic prefiguration may endow a novel with a kind of grandeur, bringing a heroic dimension to the ordinary, what is just as likely is that the mythic parallel will be employed for its comic or anachronistic value. As M. M. Bakhtin suggests in describing a dialogue between the epic and the novel (which is also appropriate to the dialogue between a myth and a mythological novel), the laughter and comedy that are found in the latter destroy the distancing effect found in the former. The Victorian distancing of *The Scarlet Letter* keeps us at arm's length, whereas Updike, in his trilogy, brings the story up close to "where one can finger it familiarly." Destroying the mythic distance, Updike makes the characters familiar and human, and he satirizes the earlier story by creating humorous parallels: in *A Month of Sundays* the Dimmesdale figure is a masturbator; in *Roger's Version* the Chillingworth figure is a dull academic who concocts pornographic fantasies about his wife and the Dimmesdale figure; and in *S.* the Hester figure falls in love with a religious man, an Indian guru who fraudulently turns out to be a Jew from Massachusetts. In what he refers to as his "three religious comedies," Updike not only deflates the mythic size of *The Scarlet Letter*, but he also pro-

21. Ibid., 228.

duces a picture of contemporary reality, reminiscent of the work of Nabokov and even the early John Barth, in which parody itself becomes "the most accurate rendering of reality."[22]

One should note that although his humor is seldom discussed, Updike had as his earliest models the *New Yorker* humorists James Thurber, E. B. White, and Robert Benchley, and his first ambition was to join their ranks: "As a boy I had hoarded pennies to buy Thurber's books, and owned them all; he was for me the brightest star in that galaxy of New York wits I yearned to emulate, however dimly." At Harvard, Updike passed through his apprenticeship as a cartoonist, writer, and editor of the *Lampoon*, where he indulged his "romantic weakness for gags," with his own "specialty" being "Chinese jokes." And as a published writer, Updike has exhibited comic irony in much of his writing, particularly in his light verse, early essays (some of which he called "Parodies"), and two volumes documenting the travels of the Jewish-American writer Henry Bech. As he states in a recent interview, "I do notice that my later stuff is funny," and his trilogy is to some extent a fulfillment of an early desire to be a humorist.[23]

In further regard to the uniqueness of the mythological novel, one must consider point of view. How aware or unaware is the narrator of the fact that he is retelling a well-known myth? Sarah Worth in *S.* is narrating an updated version of *The Scarlet Letter,* yet she gives no indication that she is aware of what she is doing. Though she is highly attentive to her Puritan past and continually alludes to the fact that she is responsible for every word on the page, she appears oblivious to the *Scarlet Letter* parallels and allusions. In fact, all three narrators in Updike's trilogy, though clever and deceptive, remain unaware of the *Scarlet Letter* parallel. And though the main effect of this unawareness is irony, it also arouses the contention, however artificial, that such a myth, by recurring without even the awareness of the characters or the narrator, is so deeply ingrained in our social unconscious that we repeat it without knowing, thus making it archetypal.

---

22. Ibid., 70, 89; Bakhtin, *The Dialogic Imagination*, 23; Updike, Letter to the author, January 26, 1989; Vickery, *Myths and Texts*, 185.

23. Updike, "On Meeting Writers," 4; Updike, Interview with Charles Thomas Samuels, 429; Updike, Interview with Rothstein, "Woman's Viewpoint."

Point of view takes on a heightened significance in Updike's novels because of the fact that we are not dealing with a single mythological novel but with three of them, each offering a separate version of a story. And though the contemporary stories of Thomas Marshfield (Dimmesdale, in *A Month of Sundays*), Roger Lambert (Chillingworth, in *Roger's Version*), and Sarah Worth (Hester, in *S.*) appear to have few if any points of intersection, the prefigurative story that each retells is a story that they all hold in common, *The Scarlet Letter*. In retelling *The Scarlet Letter* from a triadic point of view, Updike continues in a mode that was first apparent in his short story "Four Sides of One Story," a contemporary, four-sided retelling of Tristan and Iseult, which Updike refers to as possibly "my subconscious precursor" for the trilogy.[24] In both "Four Sides" and the trilogy, Updike deconstructs an earlier tale and demonstrates how a story operates as a sort of vortex made up of the voices of the characters involved. This relates to Bakhtin's concept of dialogics, in which an author's vision unfolds as a polyphony of distinct voices in conflict with one another. In breaking down the *Scarlet Letter* myth into its component voices, Updike also provides a narrative soapbox for each of Hawthorne's rather private characters to speak directly to the reader. Updike reverses Hawthorne's verbal retention by allowing Hester, Dimmesdale, and Chillingworth the opportunity finally to tell their own stories, with whatever words and in as frank a manner as they so choose.

A final word regarding methodology seems necessary at this point, particularly for those who in the pages ahead may be anticipating (and will be thus disappointed by not finding) a study of myth. The ensuing chapters will attempt primarily to analyze the dialogue between Updike's texts and Hawthorne's *Scarlet Letter*. Since there are a great many parallels and allusions that have not yet been accounted for or analyzed in the trilogy, this study will be more concerned than most with intertextual issues of plot and theme (what precisely is happening and what it means). One of the purposes of this introduction has been to establish *The Scarlet Letter* as an American myth and to understand what issues and questions revolve around its mythic presence. Once that has been

24. Letter to the author, August 14, 1991.

established, and once a foundation has been laid for understanding the nature of the dialogue between a myth and a contemporary mythic narrative (reader expectation, fragmentation and condensation, parody, narrative awareness, and point of view), the dialogue itself can be analyzed. Thus, the following chapters will attempt to understand precisely how Updike is responding to Hawthorne, and how Updike is attempting to redefine, by contemporary standards, the relationship in America between individual and community.

As far as the specific chapters of this text are concerned, Chapter 1 discusses *A Month of Sundays*, or "Dimmesdale's version." In casting Marshfield as Dimmesdale, Updike focuses upon the verbal abilities of the minister. Possessing the "Tongue of Flame," Dimmesdale is a gifted speaker who finds himself repeatedly in pulpits and on balconies and scaffolds, speaking and preaching to the people of Boston. Updike's Marshfield is equally adept with language, and his pulpit is his diary, through which he displays his verbal powers in an oratorical performance par excellence. Yet Marshfield's sermonizing greatly differs from Dimmesdale's. Parodic and humorous, Marshfield delivers a comic performance filled with wordplay and silly puns. And whereas Dimmesdale's speech emphasizes concealment and retention, Marshfield is voluble, displaying a post-Freudian desire to emote. Through the voice of Marshfield, Updike is calling into question Dimmesdale's mock piety and attempting to revise America's understanding of Christianity, divorcing it from the oppression of social ethics.

Chapter 2 deals with *Roger's Version*. Chillingworth, the learned and bookish doctor, finds a contemporary counterpart in Updike's Roger Lambert, an equally bookish doctor of divinity at what appears to be Harvard. Much as *The Scarlet Letter* focuses itself upon the act of seeing—Chillingworth recognizing his adulterous wife in the opening scene, Dimmesdale witnessing the falling meteor, Chillingworth eyeing the bare bosom of the sleeping Dimmesdale, the townspeople observing the various scaffold scenes, and a vocabulary that emphasizes vision and perspective—Updike appropriates Hawthorne's concern by essentially making *Roger's Version* a discourse on visualization. Like Chillingworth before him, Roger Lambert is a voyeur. He delights in seeing into and through the eyes of others and, in the process, manipulating the lives of others. Having reached the staleness of middle age, Roger feeds off of others in an attempt to inject new energy into his life so that he may literally see anew.

Chapter 3 discusses the epistolary novel *S.* Of the novels of the trilogy, *S.* is the most concerned with the American experiment of dissent, separation, and heroic struggle in an effort to rebuild the world. In retelling Hester's story, Updike pays particular attention to the notion of shedding skins, transforming the self, and even the question of whether the self can be changed. One of the central issues in Updike's trilogy is the American self, divided and unhappy, struggling to re-form and reconceive itself. And to a large degree, the crisis of self arises out of the problematic state of America. Though America is no longer beleaguered by the gray, iron men of Hawthorne's sensibility, a new monster menaces the land: an "ease and comfort," a "milky human kindness" that lacks vibrancy and physical intensity (*MS*, 50, 59). America appears to have lost something vital to its existence, and Sarah Worth speaks of "the curious correct emptiness of our lives as if half the normal human baggage had been left back in Suffolk, England, in 1630" (*S.*, 244). In *A Month of Sundays*, Thomas Marshfield addresses more extensively this notion of "lost baggage" and how it applies to the American self: "Somewhere . . . an American mystery was circumscribed, having to do with *knowing*, with acceptance of body by soul, with recovery of some baggage lost in the Atlantic crossing, with some viral thrill at the indignity of incarnation, with some monstrous and gorgeous otherness the female and male genitals meet in one another" (*MS*, 134–35). In America, Updike is stating, we have lost touch with the corporeal and become less than whole.

In attempting to transform and reconceive themselves, Updike's protagonists follow the path of the hero as outlined in Joseph Campbell's *The Hero with a Thousand Faces:* "a separation from the world, a penetration to some source of power, and a life-enhancing return."[25] Spiritually dead in their middle-class lives, Updike's heroes cross the threshold and journey into regions unknown, primarily the desert, in hopes of rebirth. And though it is ambiguous as to how successful they finally are, or even whether they can

25. *Hero with a Thousand Faces*, 35.

return to their former lives, it is reasonably safe to say that they have become transfigured in the process. Like Arthur Dimmesdale, Roger Chillingworth, and Hester Prynne before them, Updike's Thomas Marshfield, Roger Lambert, and Sarah Worth attempt to renew their lives by journeying to the American wilderness, a geographical and psychological region where old skins are shed so that new ones may be formed.

ONE

A Month of Sundays
Minister with the
Tongue of Flame

Published in 1975, *A Month of Sundays* has remained one of Updike's more neglected works, though presumably this will change now that the work must be viewed as the initial volume in a trilogy of rewritings of *The Scarlet Letter.* Greeted unenthusiastically, the novel was criticized mostly as disappointing self-indulgence by a very gifted writer. Gary Waller has since pointed out that this novel in particular offers what is both "fascinating" and "irritating" about Updike, as the writing hovers between "stylistic brilliance" and "self-indulgence." Updike himself, who has admitted to favoring the book as he would a "neglected child," implied perhaps his own carelessness when he stated in 1986 that "I gave Dimmesdale's version, in an of course updated, askew, and irresponsible way, in *A Month of Sundays.*"[1] Though excessive and self-indulgent, the novel is nonetheless more self-consciously clever and playfully complex, more reflexively postmodern, than Updike's earlier productions. And there is much that has been overlooked, both in relation to and independent of Hawthorne's *Scarlet Letter.*

A Month of Sundays is delivered in diary form by the Reverend Thomas Marshfield, who is living in temporary exile at a motel for ministers-gone-astray in the Arizona desert. Like his precursor, Arthur Dimmesdale, Marshfield is a Protestant minister from Massachusetts who has become entangled in adultery with his female

---

1. Waller, "Stylus Dei," 269; Updike, Interview with Richard Burgin, "A Conversation with John Updike," 10; Updike, "A 'Special Message' [*Roger's Version*]," 858.

parishioners. Over the course of his thirty-one days in exile, Marshfield preaches, jokes, confesses, analyzes, criticizes, pleads, and puns, accumulating enough diary entries to fill a book. For the most part the entries describe the series of events and the sort of uncontrolled adulterous behavior that landed him in exile in the first place. Indefatigable in his desire to brandish his rhetorical skills, Marshfield courts and flirts with his reader, who increasingly becomes a larger presence in the novel and is ultimately the object of his seductive interests. And the novel's fitting crescendo is Marshfield's achieved coitus with his dearly beloved reader, the motel manageress, Ms. Prynne.

There are three interwoven plot strands in the novel, all of which connect to the text's central concern: the act of writing. The first and most obvious strand is Marshfield's therapy, his effort "to work out a stain" and return to society.[2] Utilizing a literary mode common to New England preachers, particularly Puritans, Marshfield turns to microscopic self-examination in order to measure his actions and transform his life. However, in Marshfield's case, journal keeping is not voluntary: his "keepers" have organized a program of recuperation in which he is directed to write "ad libidum" so as to move toward self-knowledge and an eventual return to society. Marshfield is both drawn toward and resistant to such therapy. The second strand, which does not unfold until midway through the novel, is Marshfield's attempt to seduce Ms. Prynne. Through his writing, which he imagines her to be reading, Marshfield hopes to charm, delight, and bed the matronly manageress. This strand, dominating the latter pages of the novel, also offers the purest allegory that can be found in Updike, as Marshfield's seduction of Ms. Prynne represents, among other things, the writer's seduction and penetration of the reader. The third and final strand, which to a degree integrates the other two, is the ongoing dialogue between *A Month of Sundays* and *The Scarlet Letter.* Through such a dialogue Updike reexamines not only the characters and themes found in Hawthorne's novel, but also the nature of the contemporary American self as it continues to struggle toward transformation and renewal.

The glue holding these three strands together, and effectively the

2. Updike, Interview with Donald J. Greiner, "Updike on Hawthorne," 3.

focus of the novel, is Marshfield's verbal performance. Having been brought to the desert and placed in an isolated motel room, Marshfield faces one essential task: to write. His therapy and recovery depend upon his ability to verbalize, and his eventual courtship and seduction of Ms. Prynne indulge and reflect upon his rhetorical skills. Even the key to the correspondence between Marshfield and Dimmesdale (and Hawthorne himself in "The Custom-House" sketch) can best be understood in regard to the act of verbalization, since all of these figures seek catharsis and spiritual renewal through their verbal performances.

Whereas verbalization takes the form of written speech for Marshfield, for Dimmesdale verbalization is primarily through spoken speech. Though Dimmesdale is pictured writing his Election Sermon in an inspirational frenzy, it is more common in *The Scarlet Letter* to see him in pulpits and on balconies and scaffolds, speaking and preaching to the people of Boston. A magnificent speaker, Dimmesdale possesses "the Tongue of Flame," the power of "addressing the whole human brotherhood in the heart's native language": "The young pastor's voice was tremulously sweet, rich, deep, and broken. The feeling that it so evidently manifested, rather than the direct purport of the words, caused it to vibrate within all hearts, and brought the listeners into one accord of sympathy" (*SL*, 142, 67). As a minister, Dimmesdale has a duty to speak to the people, to minister to their fears and needs, to stand before them and provide for them through the use of language. And certainly in comparison to Chillingworth and Hester, Dimmesdale is the most verbal, the character who most relies upon public speech.

In his initial appearance Dimmesdale is called upon by his superiors to rectify an element of social disorder, Hester's adultery, by acting in the capacity for which he is best suited: speaking to the public. Here, in front of the crowd gathered to witness Hester Prynne's humiliation, the Reverend John Wilson, the eldest clergyman of Boston, calls upon Dimmesdale to speak: "Good Master Dimmesdale . . . the responsibility of this woman's soul lies greatly with you. It behooves you, therefore, to exhort her to repentance, and to confession, as a proof and consequence thereof" (*SL*, 66). It becomes an ironic moment as Dimmesdale utilizes clever language and veiled speech, representative of his divided self: "Hester Prynne

. . . thou hearest what this good man says, and seest the account-
ability under which I labor. If thou feelest it to be for thy soul's
peace . . . I charge thee to speak out the name of thy fellow-sinner
and fellow-sufferer!" (*SL*, 67). Speech is a crucial act for Dimmesdale not only because he is a minister, but also because he is guilty
of an act that he feels demands public disclosure through speech.
Tempted and yet fearful of speaking truthfully, Dimmesdale divides and tortures himself, employing a language of doublespeak.

Having entered the pulpit repeatedly with the intention of confessing the truth, of utilizing speech to regain physical and spiritual health, Dimmesdale can never manage to deliver the actual
words:

> More than once, . . . he had cleared his throat, and drawn in the
> long, deep, and tremulous breath, which, when sent forth again,
> would come burdened with the black secret of his soul. More than
> once—nay, more than a hundred times—he had actually spoken!
> Spoken! . . . The minister well knew—subtle, but remorseful hypo-
> crite that he was!—the light in which his vague confession would be
> viewed. . . . He had spoken the very truth, and transformed it into
> the veriest falsehood. (*SL*, 143–44)

There is a sexual intensity to how Dimmesdale frantically arouses
and tortures himself, and as we shall see, there is a direct correspondence between Dimmesdale's final verbal performance on the
scaffold and Marshfield's ultimate verbal performance of seducing
and entering his reader.

In re-creating Dimmesdale in the character of Marshfield, Updike has chosen to focus upon the role of the minister as speaker, or
in this case, writer. Like Dimmesdale, Marshfield has been asked
by his superiors to address, with words, a social wrong: "My keepers have set before me a sheaf of blank sheets—a month's worth, in
their estimation. Sullying them is to be my sole therapy" (*MS*, 3).
And like Dimmesdale, Marshfield is eloquent and gifted with language, though the effect of his words is more clever and playful
than emotional: "The month is to be one of recuperation—as I
think of it, 'retraction,' my condition being officially diagnosed as
one of 'distraction.' Perhaps the opposite of 'dis' is not 're' but the
absence of any prefix, by which construal I am spiritual brother to
those broken-boned athletes who must spend a blank month, amid

white dunes and midnight dosages, in 'traction'" (*MS*, 3-4). Employing significant rhetorical skills and indulging in word games and verbal prestidigitation, Marshfield proves to be a clever and deceptive speaker like his precursor. When a jealous husband confronts him, demanding to know whether he has had an affair with the man's wife, Marshfield, guilty of innumerous sexual acts with the wife but unable ultimately to maintain an erection in her presence, responds: "'I swear, solemnly, that I never'—the word had to be exact—'fucked your good wife'" (*MS*, 176). Like Dimmesdale, Marshfield is adept at manipulating language, speaking truthfully and accurately while yet maintaining deception.

As a writer, Marshfield initially resists the impulse to deliver himself on paper: "I feel myself warming to this, which is not my intent. Let my distraction remain intractable" (*MS*, 4). Depreciating the act of writing as solipsistic, he finds the process of putting pen to paper, or finger to typewriter in his case, to be exhausting and depressing. He also distrusts therapy as a kind of magic designed to return him to that dull being he was before the adultery began: "Is this the end of therapy, a reshouldering of ambiguity, rote performance, daily grits, hollow vows, stale gratifications, receding illusions?" (*MS*, 213). Yet he cannot resist the pleasures of writing, delighting in the sense of play and in the opportunity for free and creative expression. In addition, he is attracted to the power that a writer acquires through manipulating and reinterpreting experience, and also to the challenge of seducing the reader.

Before proceeding I would like to clarify a point in regard to verbalization. As Father Ong and others tell us, there are indeed distinctions to be made between acts of writing and speaking; however, this study does not attempt to engage that question in any degree of depth. After all, Marshfield and Dimmesdale are literary characters, and ultimately there can be no real question of orality. However, as characters operating within a given literary text, there is indeed a distinction between the modes of verbalization that Dimmesdale and Marshfield utilize. In *The Scarlet Letter* we read both the actual and reported speech of Dimmesdale, yet he remains a distant figure; we, as readers, linger on the outside, with only occasional glimpses of the interior life of the character. In *A Month of Sundays*, however, Updike removes that distance, plunging us directly into the first-person confessional mode, in which we witness the interior and hidden side of Marshfield/ Dimmesdale. By utilizing the diary as his subgenre, Updike provides the untold story; Marshfield/Dimmesdale speaks directly and frankly to the reader. Or does he? As we shall see, Marshfield, in his so-called private writing, puts on as much of a verbal performance as Dimmesdale does in his public speaking (though there are indeed differences in the content and tone of what they say). Interestingly enough, on this occasion and within the confines of a literary text, literacy and orality, personal writing and public speech, prove to be not so different; in each case there is a public performance marked by equivocation, dissemblance, and manipulation.

The persistent conflict in Marshfield's (and Dimmesdale's) mind, between socially acceptable behavior and passionate gesture, finds expression in language. In *A Month of Sundays*, there is undoubtedly a strong relationship between writing and adultery, and as John T. Matthews suggests, "Marshfield comes to understand that writing repeats . . . adultery" as it tries "to cure it." Writing allows another form for Marshfield's seductive and desirous inclinations. Not only does he literally adulterate himself by becoming both narrator and character, but also the actual process of writing provides the same type of creative release experienced in adultery. Tony Tanner points out that the chaos of adultery can be related to the chaos of language. He suggests that "puns and ambiguities are to common language what adultery and perversion are to 'chaste' (i.e., socially orthodox) sexual relations."[3] Marshfield's narrative— loose, comic, colloquial, sexually explicit, and playful—adopts a singular form of speech that creatively breaks away from ordinary, conventional language. In addition, just as adultery undermines social order, law, and authority, Marshfield's writing questions and subverts the authority of the text itself and creates a level of uncertainty and ambiguity: "Or perhaps these words were never spoken, I made them up, to relieve and rebuke the silence of this officiously chaste room" (*MS*, 33). Much like adultery, writing creates an awakening of energy, which can lead to the forging of a new kind of expression. As such, both adultery and writing offer a

---

3. Matthews, "Intertextuality and Originality: Hawthorne, Faulkner, Updike," 156; see also, Matthews, "Word as Scandal"; and Tanner, *Adultery in the Novel*, 53.

passage to self-discovery and redemption, while embodying the temptation and freedom of passionate expression.

Much as Dimmesdale wavers between confessing and concealing, Marshfield vacillates between indulging and resisting the confessional act of therapeutic writing. As Marshfield describes it, he has been led into "temptation" by his "keepers," who have asked him to "sully" a "sheaf of blank sheets" (note the adulterous allusion). Desiring to retain his sense of self, Marshfield vows that the adulterous soul he has recently been "will not be forgotten, though all the forces of institutional therapeutics be brought to bear upon me" (*MS*, 11). Convinced that his therapy is a ploy by his keepers to lure him back to acceptable communal behavior, Marshfield resists. Yet ultimately the temptation to write is too overwhelming. Through the example of his father, a minister who spent his Saturdays typing sermons, Marshfield has come to see a correspondence between the act of writing and the act of seduction: "On Saturdays he would type—ejaculations of clatter after long foreplay of silent agony" (*MS*, 18). And when Marshfield describes in his writing the naked body of his church organist, Alicia Crick, he becomes so stimulated that he masturbates, thus deflating his writing of its original force and intensity: "I shouldn't have done it, for now my hymn to my mistress will be limp and piecemeal, tapped out half by a hand still tremulous and smelling of venerable slime" (*MS*, 34). Marshfield manipulates his language as if engaging in foreplay, both with himself and with his reader. Yet as the sexual momentum of his writing builds, he must resist the temptation of relief or else his writing will lose its narrative potency: "Her clinging to me naked, at the head of the stairs . . . still so moves this abandoning heart that a less tension-loving typist would be driven again to the ruggy floor of his padded cell" (*MS*, 36).

Marshfield's effort to sustain sexual intensity is reminiscent of Dimmesdale, whose story can be read, at least in sexual terms, as a heroic effort to withhold his dark secret until finally releasing it in a climactic burst. Dimmesdale remarks that the heart must hold onto "the secrets that may be buried" within, and that on the day when finally revealed, a tremendous relief will be realized: "such an outpouring, O, what a relief" (*SL*, 131–32). Yet before that final ecstatic burst, Dimmesdale increases the pain, agony, and pleasure of his situation by what D. H. Lawrence interprets as an exercise in self-flagellation: "He has a good time all by himself torturing his body, whipping it, piercing it with thorns, macerating himself. It's a form of masturbation. He wants to get a mental grip on his body."[4] Although it is his sexuality that Dimmesdale is attempting to conceal and punish himself for, his very effort at concealment and self-flagellation tends to increase the sexual intensity of his situation.

As is true in both *The Scarlet Letter* and *A Month of Sundays*, the voice or vocal organ represents and expresses a person's sexuality. When Dimmesdale delivers his Election Sermon, "an irresistible feeling" draws Hester to listen and "bring the whole sermon to her ears": "This vocal organ was in itself a rich endowment; insomuch that a listener, comprehending nothing of the language in which the preacher spoke, might still have been swayed to and fro by the mere tone and cadence. Like all other music, it breathed passion and pathos, and emotions high or tender, in a tongue native to the human heart" (*SL*, 242–43). Earlier, when the dazed Dimmesdale returns from his forest meeting with Hester, aroused no doubt by her physical attractions, he attempts through vocalization to release his pent-up erotic desire. After resisting a series of temptations, including that of teaching "some very wicked words to a knot of little Puritan children," he returns to his room and throws himself into his Election Sermon "with such an impulsive flow of thought and emotion, that he fancied himself inspired" (*SL*, 225).

Marshfield is a good deal more aware of the sexual power of both language and voice. In writing of his mother, he recalls most vividly her beautiful voice: "I see that my mother's singing voice was, for me, her sex; that her hoarseness I transferred in my childish innocence to her lower mouth, which was, as I stood small beside her in the pew, at the level of my mouth; that I equate noise with vitality; that silence, chastity, and death fascinate me with one face; that Alicia's power over the organ keyboards was part of her power over me" (*MS*, 20). Marshfield is attracted by Alicia's boldness, both in her music and in her sexuality. Yet ultimately, Alicia, a player of organs, attempts to take over the Sunday services with her music, and Marshfield is forced to dismiss her. Both voice and language carry a suggestion of sexual power, and later, when a jealous and angry Gerry Harlow confronts Marshfield, it is

4. *Studies*, 96.

in regard to the vocal intimacy that Marshfield has shared with Harlow's wife: "'She's talked freely to you'" (*MS*, 176).

To this point similarities have been drawn between Dimmesdale and Marshfield according to how they use language and speech. Yet as speakers and as personalities, they are quite different. Dimmesdale is pious, reverent, and serious; Marshfield is witty, mocking, and radically improper. Marshfield's diary is parodic and humorous, filled with wordplay and bawdy puns. He even discloses information about his penis size and bowel movements. Updike's treatment of Dimmesdale stands in contrast to Michael Davitt Bell's contention that if *The Scarlet Letter* were told from Dimmesdale's point of view, it "might sound . . . like a tale by Poe."[5] Updike has recast Dimmesdale as a prankster and a clown. The question is why.

Updike is of course parodying Dimmesdale. Sexual attitudes in America have changed drastically since 1850, and Dimmesdale's sexual neuroses appear humorous today. Yet parody answers the question only partially. Updike has chosen to put his own personal stamp on Hawthorne's minister. Whereas Hawthorne surrounds his minister with shadows, secrets, and mystery, Updike opts for a less haunted and disturbed characterization, and one that has more in common with his own sensibility. Described by one friend as an "utterly entertaining, frivolous beyond belief, and wildly funny man," Updike appears to get a good deal of himself into Marshfield.[6] And interestingly enough, the most entertaining and clownish of all Updike's characters tend to be those "fatherly" spiritual figures who wield some type of communal religious power: Freddy Thorne as a priest figure in *Couples*, Darryl Van Horne as the devil in *The Witches of Eastwick*, and Marshfield. A "spiritual man" himself and a "card-carrying Episcopalian," Updike is apparently making an effort to transform the nature of the "religious man" in America.[7] Removing the drabness and dust from the tomb of American Christianity, Updike endows his religious figures with a bold sense of humor, a mocking anxiety, and an ecstatic appreciation for physical as well as spiritual life.

In addition, Updike transforms Dimmesdale's verbal retentive-

---

5. *The Development of American Romance: The Sacrifice of Relation*, 178.
6. "Notes from the Editors," 18.
7. Updike, Interview with Rothstein, "Woman's Viewpoint."

ness into Marshfield's volubility. Whereas Dimmesdale strives
to keep dangerous thoughts and words within, Marshfield desires
to tell everything: "I saw my own phallus erect up to my navel.
She spread her legs quickly" (*MS*, 157). This distinction between
Dimmesdale's retention and Marshfield's volubility points not only
to the difference between Hawthorne's shadowy and repressive
romanticism and Updike's clinically frank realism, but also and
more significantly to the internal warfare between body and soul.
Dimmesdale, holding his secret and passion within, allows his
Calvinistic soul to eat away at and destroy his body. Marshfield,
on the other hand, with a sexual frankness and post-Freudian desire to emote, attempts to reconcile body and soul. As we later
shall see, the voluble Marshfield offers to his readers, and seeks for
himself, a revised understanding of Christianity that stresses a
good-natured tolerance and appreciation of the corporeal.

Since the tone and language of Marshfield's speech is so different from that of Dimmesdale, it becomes necessary to trace more
specific influences. Kierkegaard and Barth, who figure prominently in Marshfield's theology, may also play a role in his prose
style. George W. Hunt explains that "one of the attractive features
of both Kierkegaard and Barth is that each speaks with a distinc-
tively *dramatic* voice—Barth in the preacher's tone, Kierkegaard
in the poet's or novelist's tone. Thus their writings address the reader
with a sense of personal urgency and ever make use of dramatic
techniques such as irony, hyperbole, repetition of phrase, and the
allusive aside." Marshfield himself expresses his attraction to Barth
the writer: "I did not become a Barthian in blank recoil, but in
positive love of Barth's voice, his wholly masculine, wholly informed, wholly unfrightened prose" (*MS*, 24–25). As shall become
visible throughout the trilogy, Barth is not only a verbal influence,
but he is also the major theological influence. For those unfamiliar with the neoorthodox Swiss, the central concept in Updike's
utilization of Barthian theology is that God is "Wholly Other,"
that there is an abyss between the human and the divine that no
bridge can cross.[8] Such an abyss emphasizes the tremendous maj-

8. Hunt, *Secret Things*, 18; Karl Barth, *The Word of God and the Word of
Man*, 24. Father Hunt's book is the best available in discussing theology in
Updike. For further discussion on Barth's influence in Updike see Frederick

esty of God and the insignificance of human events, human deeds. Ethics becomes downgraded in Barth's theology, and faith in divine revelation is made central. Updikean protagonists have long embraced Barthian thinking and have sought a form of Christianity more in touch with the Incarnation than with so-called Christian ethics.

Nabokov and Lawrence must also be invoked when discussing vocal influences upon Marshfield. With his verbal playfulness and dexterity, his lurid sexual intensity and anxious mocking voice, Nabokov's Humbert Humbert is the most obvious precursor: "Lolita, light of my life, fire of my loins. My sin, my soul. Lo-lee-ta: the tip of the tongue taking a trip of three steps down the palate to tap, at three on the teeth. Lo. Lee. Ta." *Lolita*, in fact, is Nabokov's effort at retelling *The Scarlet Letter.* Not only does he employ a fictional editor and foreword to explain how the text was produced, mirroring Hawthorne's "Custom-House" narrator, but also he parodies Hawthorne's final moral advice, "Be true," with his own double-edged counsel, "Be true to your Dick." In addition, both *The Scarlet Letter* and *Lolita* are centrally concerned with passionate love that transgresses social custom and law. As for Lawrence, the narrative voice that he utilizes in the chapter "The Holy Family," from *Fantasia of the Unconscious*, bears a remarkable similarity to that of Marshfield. Not only does Lawrence speak in that same colloquial, comic tone, which calls attention to itself and questions its own means of narration, but also he employs what Hawthorne refers to as "the antique fashion" of addressing the narrator: "There's more in you, dear reader, than meets the eye. What, don't you believe it?"[9] Perhaps Updike's debt to Lawrence extends beyond even the scope of Lawrence's essay on *The Scarlet Letter* to an appropriation of the loose, colloquial, and ironic style that Lawrence employs in a good deal of his essay writing.

One final influence to consider in assessing Marshfield the writer is that of Hawthorne's narrator in the "Custom-House." Though

Crews, "Mr. Updike's Planet"; William H. Pritchard and George Hunsinger, "Updike's Version"; and Updike, "To the Tram Halt Together."

9. Nabokov, *Lolita*, 11; Hawthorne, "Preface," *The Marble Faun*, 1; Lawrence, *Fantasia of the Unconscious*, 26.

Marshfield resembles Hawthorne's narrator less in voice, there is much similarity in regard to situation. Alienated from his contemporaries and a shamed outcast, the narrator of "The Custom-House" resembles Marshfield in that both of these "writers" spend much of their time "fearfully alone" in solitary rooms, have been tarnished by scandals within their communities, can modulate their voices to switch rapidly from anxiety to mockery and anger, are self-conscious about their roles as writers, turn to writing as a means of self-discovery, and fear that they are losing their imaginative and creative energies by working in societal institutions. Within the two novels, we witness how each becomes a writer and how each finds an outlet and a mode of therapy within the act of writing.

Since the novel's title, *A Month of Sundays*, and its epigraphs fail to allude to *The Scarlet Letter*, it is possible to pass through much of the first diary entry unaware of any parallel to Hawthorne. Though we are informed immediately that our protagonist is a disgraced minister, the first specific allusion, limned in Hawthornesque ambiguity, arises from Marshfield's description of the motel's manageress: "a large lady. . . . Named, if my ears, still plugged with jet-hum, deceived me not, Ms. Prynne" (*MS*, 6). The ambiguity continues when we learn that Ms. Prynne is hardly the beauty with "dark and abundant hair, so glossy that it threw off the sunshine with a gleam" (*SL*, 53). Rather, she is a stern, matronly manageress with the "face of a large, white, inexplicably self-congratulating turtle" (*MS*, 6). The situation is made more complicated several chapters later when we learn that Marshfield is married, and to a woman née Chillingworth; Dimmesdale, of course, never married. Marshfield then goes on to explain how his adulterous descent began with his parish organist, Alicia Crick. Is she the Hester figure in the novel, or is Ms. Prynne? And why is the novel situated in the Arizona desert instead of Boston? And where is Pearl? One begins to wonder whether the *Scarlet Letter* parallel has any larger purpose than humor and parody.

As stated earlier, one must not expect to find exact precursors in Hawthorne's novel for every event and characterization in *A Month of Sundays*. Updike is free to use *The Scarlet Letter* as loosely as he chooses. If scenes, ideas, and even characters from Hawthorne's novel are ignored in Updike's retelling, that is not necessarily problematic. Yet if Updike's novel is going to stand as a successful retelling of and comment upon *The Scarlet Letter*, then the reader must be able to find substantial connections between the two texts, between the myth and the contemporary retelling. For instance, in *A Month of Sundays*, Marshfield describes himself masturbating. Though no exact parallel exists in *The Scarlet Letter*, Marshfield's masturbation can be linked to Dimmesdale's self-flagellation. As Lawrence suggests, both are attempts by the mind to control the body, and both are solipsistic acts designed to entertain and stimulate the self. [10]

Though not immediately apparent, *A Month of Sundays'* time-scheme and place are significant in relation to *The Scarlet Letter.* Marshfield states that he is writing "at some point in the time of Richard Nixon's unravelling" (*MS*, 3). The mere mention of Nixon and Watergate reminds one that the same problems facing the Puritan Commonwealth—infidelity, deception, hypocrisy—persist in America of the early 1970s. America is still the failed "Utopia" of Hawthorne's text, and public figures such as Nixon and Marshfield continue to hide their nasty secrets and to lead double lives. The political scandal of Watergate even finds vague echoes in Hawthorne's own political scandal as described in "The Custom-House." Though Surveyor Hawthorne hardly shares President Nixon's level of guilt, he nevertheless has been affected and marred by a political controversy, and to some degree he too has been exposed to that style of intense and unforgiving public scrutiny so common in American culture.

Much as the novel's time scheme is neither desultory nor insignificant, the same is true of the novel's setting: the desert. Both Marshfield and Sarah Worth of S. journey to the Arizona desert in hopes of spiritual illumination. The desert is the topos of enlightenment and of redemption, and it provides a retreat from the civilized world. Perhaps the final wilderness available in the vast reaches of America, the desert is where Marshfield can go to escape civilization, much as Hester and Dimmesdale can escape in the forest. The desert is also the place of temptation, instruction, and purification. Numerous biblical figures—Moses, Jacob, Jesus—

10. *Studies*, 96.

have found themselves "in a desert place," and most often they are there to be tested. Waterless places or deserts are notoriously a favorite habitat of demons, and in Matthew we read of Jesus being "led up by the Spirit into the Wilderness to be tempted by the devil."[11] The passage in Matthew is an illustration of Jesus' habitual refusal to give in to the devil. As mentioned earlier, Marshfield is being tempted and tested in the desert by the "blank sheets" that his superiors have placed before him: "Though the yielding is mine, the temptation belongs to others" (MS, 3).

Early on in *A Month of Sundays*, two rather significant scenes engage in dialogue with Dimmesdale's famous vigil. As described by Hawthorne, Dimmesdale would sometimes view "his own face in a looking-glass, by the most powerful light which he could throw upon it. He thus typified the constant introspection wherewith he tortured, but could not purify, himself" (SL, 145). Much like the protagonist of Hawthorne's "Monsieur du Miroir," Dimmesdale looks into the mirror to find that image, that "other," to whom he is fatefully bound for life. The scene alerts us to the disparity between interior and exterior world, body and soul, private mind and public self. And Dimmesdale is so unable to deal with what he sees in the mirror that he is soon visited by diabolic shapes and shining angels, ghosts and dead friends of youth. Dimmesdale's inability to accept and reconcile his mirror image appears to verify Updike's contention that "Hawthorne's instinctive tenet [is] that matter and spirit are inevitably at war."[12]

In *A Month of Sundays*, Marshfield, on his first morning in Arizona, goes to the mirror and sees an unfamiliar face: "It no more fits my inner light than the shade of a bridge lamp fits its bulb" (MS, 7). Like Dimmesdale, Marshfield cannot reconcile his inner and outer selves. Speaking of his outer self as a lampshade, he describes how that self fails to correspond to his inner self, the light bulb: "This lampshade. . . . This sallow sack. . . . Not mine. But it winks when I will, *wink*" (MS, 7). Reacting to this disparity between body and soul, Dimmesdale resorts to self-torture, while

11. Matt. 4:1. All biblical references are to the Oxford Revised Standard Version (New York: Oxford, 1973).
12. "Hawthorne's Creed," 77.

Marshfield mocks his condition and uses humor to begin to heal himself and prompt his reconciliation with self and world. Whereas Dimmesdale envisions mocking demons, Marshfield discovers in the mirror a pink balding spot on the crown of his head. The haunted and demonic of Hawthorne become the trivial and everyday comic in Updike.

The other scene in *A Month of Sundays* that relates to Dimmesdale's vigil concerns specifically his midnight walk to the scaffold platform. In Hawthorne's novel the impetus for Dimmesdale's nighttime wandering is to find relief. Unable to relieve his soul of its painful burden, Dimmesdale abandons his room with the intention of publicly confessing. Yet as each nocturnal opportunity for confession arises, it becomes obvious that no one will be there to witness the act, "no peril of discovery" (*SL*, 147). Dimmesdale's shriek is not as loud as he had imagined; his words to Father Wilson are "uttered only within his imagination"; and his final peal of laughter is responded to by those already aware of his "crime." Despite his desire for public confession and social reintegration, Dimmesdale's "dread of public exposure" is overwhelming. The scene ends with Pearl and Hester joining him on the scaffold, where they witness a meteor fall across the sky, which Dimmesdale interprets as a sign from a "supernatural source" of his guilt.

Marshfield's vigil is also undertaken in the hope of relief. Alicia Crick, his mistress, has left her black car parked next door to Marshfield's house at the home of his curate, Ned Bork. Certain of a sexual liaison between the two, Marshfield writhes in agony and masturbates as he watches from his bedroom window, assured that "this act of hers addressed itself to *him*" (*MS*, 11). Such language emanates from Hawthorne; Dimmesdale views the revelation of the meteor as "addressed to himself alone" (*SL*, 155). Like Dimmesdale, Marshfield has fallen into a "highly disordered mental state," in which he has "extended his egotism over the whole expanse of nature" (*SL*, 155). Unable to contain himself, Marshfield arises from bed and journeys across the lawn and into the night. Whereas Dimmesdale attired himself as if "for public worship," Marshfield is "clad in naught but the top half of pajamas striped like an untwisted candy cane" (*MS*, 10). The object of Marshfield's quest is not a scaffold, but Bork's window, where he persists in his peeping: "There, not a man's length away, basking in pinkish glow, lay a bare foot. Hers. . . . This was a foot of hers. Irrefutably. And irrefutably naked. I was stunned" (*MS*, 15). Horrified at his "visual confirmation," Marshfield returns home, noting how no sirens, angels, or comets appeared to him. Like Dimmesdale, Marshfield's faith is founded upon revelation (he is continually vigilant for a sign), but in 1973 men and women no longer read the sky for messages from God, and so there can be no cosmic revelation for Marshfield. Or can there? It would appear that for Marshfield revelation continues to exist in the corporeal world; however, Marshfield discovers revelation not in the mysterious darkness of the sky but in the spied-upon naked foot of his mistress—in other words, in woman.

Updike's depiction of this scene is one of his more Hawthornesque. To begin with, the desert-exiled Marshfield reminds the reader that he is a man writing alone in his room, an image evocative of Hawthorne's many lonely writers: the "Custom-House" narrator, Miles Coverdale of *The Blithedale Romance*, and Hawthorne himself in his upstairs bedroom at the Herbert Street house in Salem. Marshfield then presents himself as an outsider, a spectator of the lives of others, a voyeur peeking through windows. In this respect he is not unlike the numerous voyeurs one finds in Hawthorne's fiction: Coverdale, Chillingworth, Paul Pry in "Sights from a Steeple," Giovanni in "Rappaccini's Daughter," and Hawthorne himself in his *American Notebooks*. In particular Marshfield resembles Coverdale, who is not averse to spying upon the beautiful Zenobia through his hotel-room window in Boston. And if one were to search for a tone of voice in Hawthorne's fiction that comes closest to Updike's Marshfield, a natural selection would be that of Coverdale, whose voice possesses a dramatic tension and degree of unreliability, which has led Updike to refer to him as "the most actual, the most nervously alive" of all of Hawthorne's characters.[13] The point, which extends throughout the trilogy, is that Updike's intertextual dialogue with Hawthorne is not limited to *The Scarlet Letter*, though that is the primary precursor. Updike's trilogy, in a more general sense, engages in dialogue with Hawthorne's oeuvre and with his overall sensibility.

13. Ibid.

In Marshfield's vigil, Updike employs the distortion pattern of condensation: several prefigurations are condensed into the character of Marshfield. Though Marshfield is Dimmesdale, he becomes Chillingworth in this scene, assuming the role of the older, rejected husband/lover. Standing outside of Bork's window, Marshfield imagines his curate and former mistress together inside like "Hera and Zeus . . . Shakti and Shiva." Seeing how Marshfield earlier played the role of Hester (at the Arizona motel he is treated "as if in avoidance of contamination"), he now has played, if only momentarily, the roles of all three protagonists. The malleability and interchangeability of the roles within the adulterous triangle is an interesting phenomenon, indicating that during the unstable triangular course of adultery, individuals tend to live so intimately with the thoughts and actions of the other two players that their roles are liable to fluctuate and alter spontaneously. In addition, Updike demonstrates that in an adulterous configuration there is a continuous tension between the opposing impulses of transformation and stability, and that characters are liable to work in both directions.

Despite the playful allusions to Hawthorne, one wonders whether Marshfield's vigil has any greater significance, whether it is anything more than parody. As Marshfield the writer describes the actions of Marshfield the voyeur on that vigilant evening, he emphasizes that the voyeur's actions have been motivated by and are centered around not only his sexual urges but also, literally, his penis. This is significant. Updike is offering a comment upon Dimmesdale that was unavailable to Hawthorne: that Dimmesdale's problem, his torment, was literally caused by his penis. Marshfield cannot sleep because he has learned that his mistress is with another man. He masturbates, hoping that it will put him to sleep, but to no avail. He then arises from bed, sans pajama bottoms (his reason for dressing in this manner is "to facilitate masturbatory self-access"). His night journey leads him across the lawn, cluttered with sharp objects, to where he steps over a waist-high picket fence; the reader is of course alerted to the fact that his exposed genitals are in constant danger. After peeping next door and upon returning home, he falls into bed, where he thinks that his wife, "her hand surveying my coldness, was going to fumble for my penis" (*MS*, 17). Yet the "danger" of the moment passes, and the chapter ends. The significance is that Updike's version of Dimmesdale reveals him to be a man who is led primarily by his sexual instincts, represented corporeally by his penis.

Sexual desire is what releases both Dimmesdale and Marshfield from imprisonment. Dimmesdale, whose physical body is held captive by his puritanical soul, is a freer man after his rendezvous with Hester in the forest: he felt like "a prisoner just escaped from the dungeon of his own heart" (*SL*, 201). And Marshfield, repeatedly describing himself as a "slave," a "prisoner," a body "wrapped in chains," finds ecstatic release in the women of his parish. Alicia Crick, passionate and headstrong, blond and argumentative, arrives as a revelation: "This angel had come and with a blazing sword slashed the gray . . . walls of my prison" (*MS*, 32). Alicia's arrival not only revives Marshfield's stale sexual life but also reveals to him how his marriage has been a form of imprisonment. His wife, Jane Chillingworth Marshfield, epitomizes ethical goodness, the very thing that the Barthian in Marshfield despises. Imprisoned by Jane's goodness, Marshfield views his marriage as a "deep well," out of which they stare toward their impossible freedom.

Woman as physical entity is a form of revelation for these Christian ministers, who are so eagerly vigilant for signs and manifestations in the physical universe from God. For Marshfield, "Alicia in bed was a revelation" (*MS*, 33). Her physical presence, along with the sexual excitement that it stirs, signals to him the existence of a divine presence. Whereas Dimmesdale understands the flesh to be verging upon evil, Marshfield views God's presence in the exhilaration of physical stimulation. Marshfield's faith in the divine is essentially restored through the revelations of women. Alicia, however, does not turn out to be the divine answer for Marshfield. Though he realizes "naked joy, laughter, and playfulness" with her, the affair does not last. True to her surname of Crick, Alicia becomes something of a pain in the neck to Marshfield: "She berated me, disclosing all the secret ignominy our affair had visited upon her, and voicing all the shaky hardness that thirty years of being a female in America had produced" (*MS*, 82). Through his insincerity and immaturity, Marshfield has brought out the bitch in Alicia, sending her off in pursuit of other men, including his curate.

It is, in fact, Alicia's subsequent affair with Ned Bork that draws

Marshfield's attention away from Alicia to Bork: "That this pale, slight body . . . had the power of copulating with my beloved's . . . fascinated me; his very skin . . . glowed with the triumph" (*MS*, 85–86). Fiddling with his mythic adulterous triangle, Updike allows Bork to play the role of Dimmesdale, and Marshfield to assume the role of Chillingworth, the older and more knowledgeable cuckold. Much as Chillingworth and Dimmesdale are brought together through the actions of Hester, Marshfield is drawn toward Bork because of Alicia. Marshfield begins to listen to the words of Bork, whom earlier he had referred to as "a perfectly custardly confection of Jungian-Reichian soma-mysticism swimming in a soupy caramel of Tillichic, Jasperian, Bultmannish blather" (*MS*, 13). It is not that Marshfield now finds the liberal-humanism of Bork convincing, but rather that he is fascinated by the man who so insouciantly has seduced his mistress. In describing his relationship with Bork, Marshfield could just as easily be speaking for Roger Chillingworth: "I was still his superior, and my knowledge of his secret, where he had none of mine, improved my advantage. But the sum of all this was intimacy. Heaven forbid, I began to love him" (*MS*, 86). As an apparent comment upon Hawthorne's conclusion, which poses the question as to "whether hatred and love be not the same thing at bottom," Updike suggests a homoerotic element to the relationship between the Chillingworth and Dimmesdale figures (this path he will pursue more vigorously in *Roger's Version*). Though Updike's characters are decidedly heterosexual, adulterous configurations offer them the otherwise taboo pleasures of homoeroticism without the public visibility.

The primary Chillingworth figure in *A Month of Sundays* is of course "The Doctor Reverend Wesley Augustus Chillingworth," Jane's father and Marshfield's professor of ethics at divinity school. Like his precursor, Wesley Chillingworth is a man of books, a scholar who has become dull and dry from a lifetime of reading. And his ethics course epitomized for Marshfield "everything I hated about academic religion; its safe and complacent faithlessness, its empty difficulty, its transformation of the tombstones of the passionate dead into a set of hurdles for the living to leap on their way to an underpaid antique profession" (*MS*, 50). Marshfield, back in his role as Dimmesdale, is what Lawrence refers to as "the new spiritual aspirer." And Wesley Chillingworth, representing dry knowledge and the dullness of Christian ethics, is "the old order of intellect."[14] Whereas Marshfield thrives upon rebellion, Chillingworth is ordered and stoic. Marshfield, as a Barthian, reacts against the faithlessness and ethical base of Chillingworth's belief, and he resents and rebels against the inherited intellectual tradition. In fact, Marshfield goes so far as to suggest that he may have seduced Chillingworth's daughter, Jane, "as an undermining and refutation of the old polymath's theology" (*MS*, 54). He even parallels his seduction of Jane with his enrollment in her father's ethics course: "As Kant attempted to soften rationalism with categorical imperatives and *Achtung*, Jane let me caress her breast through her sweater" (*MS*, 51). Whether or not we believe that Marshfield seduced Jane so as to undermine her father, two crucial points are suggested that bear significance in much of the trilogy: first, sex and religion are intimately linked and often elicit similar emotional and physical responses; and second, the Hester figure, interchangeably a wife or a daughter, is at times a mere possession or pawn held by the older man and desired by the younger one.

In regard to the Chillingworth figure, it is also worthwhile to note that he will significantly evolve in the second volume of the trilogy, *Roger's Version*. The dry and complacent professor of *A Month of Sundays*, given only a minor role in this novel, becomes the central character and narrator of Updike's second volume. Though Roger Lambert of *Roger's Version* initially resembles Updike's earlier attempt at Chillingworth—he too is a dull professor at a divinity school (note how Updike associates Chillingworth, dullness, and academia)—he proves to be a much more lively, ironic, and interesting character. To a large degree, the difference stems from the change in perspective, affirming John Barth's point that

everyone is necessarily the hero of his own life story. *Hamlet* could be told from Polonius's point of view and called *The Tragedy of Polonius, Lord Chamberlain of Denmark*. He didn't think he was a minor character in anything, I daresay. Or suppose you're an usher in a wedding. From the groom's viewpoint he's the major character; the others play supporting parts, even the bride. From your viewpoint,

14. *Studies*, 105.

though, the wedding is a minor episode in the very interesting history of *your* life, and the bride and groom both are minor figures.[15]

When given the opportunity to tell his own story and assume the role of the main character, Roger Lambert of *Roger's Version*, though externally similar to Updike's version of Chillingworth in *A Month of Sundays*, proves to have a fascinating and intense interior life. By allowing the reader access to the inner machinations of each of Hawthorne's three protagonists, Updike surrounds the story from three points and allows each of Hawthorne's characters to assume the role of the hero.

As for the Hester figure in *A Month of Sundays*, she is fragmented, meaning that a variety of characters temporarily assume her role, including Jane Chillingworth, Alicia Crick, Frankie Harlow, and Ms. Prynne. Jane plays the role of Hester during Marshfield's courtship of her; she is the woman whom Marshfield takes from Chillingworth. The two young lovers undress and engage in sex in her upstairs room while "her father cleared his throat below." For the young Marshfield, Jane is initially an exciting sexual presence, "[pulling] me down into herself" and proving herself "alarmingly adept." Yet this is the perception of a youthful Marshfield. After they are married, Jane proves to be the essence of goodness, and Marshfield is satisfied neither physically nor spiritually. Marshfield then looks for other Hesters. Through Jane, one wonders what would have happened had Hawthorne's Hester Prynne married Dimmesdale: Would she too have become the paragon of goodness (as she actually does, to a superficial degree, in Hawthorne's novel)? Would she too have ceased to attract Dimmesdale sexually (arguments could also be made that this happens in *The Scarlet Letter*)? Updike's Jane Chillingworth demonstrates how the institution of marriage, as viewed from a male perspective, disarms a sexually attractive young woman such as Hester of her allure and renders her an "ethical and soft" wife.

Alicia Crick becomes the next Hester figure in *A Month of Sundays*, epitomizing the pleasures of the flesh. Not only is she a "sexual demon" in Marshfield's eyes, but she also forces him to realize—"scales fell from my eyes"—the truth about his marriage. Yet she too becomes a nuisance to Marshfield (one begins to wonder whether

15. *The End of the Road*, 88.

Dimmesdale felt the same about Hester), and he abandons her. Alicia represents the passionate and sexual Hester, and also the Hester who is discarded and disavowed. Through Alicia and Jane, Updike demonstrates how patriarchal society continues to project Hester's fate upon other women: the sexual and spiritual revelation soon becomes a discarded mistress/wife.

From the fleshly pleasures of Alicia, Marshfield escapes into the spirituality of Frankie Harlow. Unlike Jane and Alicia, Frankie is "a believer," and that renders Marshfield impotent: "I felt my heart spill, while my penis hung mute" (*MS*, 131). Intimidated by Frankie's unyielding faith, Marshfield interrogates and abuses the "staunch churchwoman" in an effort to dissociate her from her belief and thus stiffen his organ. Marshfield, however, is unable to reconcile the spiritual and physical with Frankie. Her religious belief and churchly posture are too desexualizing, rendering him physically impotent.

The final Hester figure in the novel is Marshfield's reader, Ms. Prynne, who may be an imagined creature of the manuscript (Marshfield refers to her once as just "Ms.," the abbreviation for *manuscript*). Perhaps he has created her to make his loneliness less miserable, his writing more stimulating. Or she may be a true flesh-and-blood character. Whichever the case, Marshfield's seduction of her represents the writer's seduction and penetration of the reader, and their final moment of coitus serves as a fitting literary and sexual climax. As a character, real or imagined, Ms. Prynne is a matronly fortress who moves with a "patrolling step"; "inflexible and chaste," she appears inseduceable. Updike's Ms. Prynne is a figure of authority who assumes power over weakened and fallen religious men, and she forces the reader to reconsider the relationship between Hawthorne's Hester and Dimmesdale in regard to the role of power, control, and authority. In addition, because she is the *only* woman at the desert motel, the only object for Marshfield's heterosexual passions, Updike is suggesting that all women, from a male perspective, potentially play the role of Hester.

In assuming the role of the inseduceable reader, Updike's Ms. Prynne reminds us once again of how significant verbalization is to the Marshfield/Dimmesdale figure. As a contemporary Dimmesdale, Marshfield attempts to seduce Ms. Prynne through language. Through his words, which penetrate into her mind, Marshfield hopes to enter her body. As a comment upon *The Scarlet Letter,* Updike is reminding us of how Dimmesdale's female parishioners found him and his language so sexually appealing: "The virgins of his church grew pale around him, victims of a passion so imbued with religious sentiment that they imagined it to be all religion, and brought it openly, in their white bosoms, as their most acceptable sacrifice before the altar" (*SL,* 142). For ministers like Marshfield and Dimmesdale, words offer entrance, both sexually and spiritually, into the lives of others. Updike's Marshfield compels us to reconsider Hawthorne's Dimmesdale: Were Dimmesdale's magnificent sermons written as vehicles for seducing female parishioners, in particular Hester Prynne? Did Dimmesdale imagine Hester to be his listener/reader when he composed his sermons? And in characterizing Ms. Prynne as a firm, serious, and demanding reader, is Updike suggesting perhaps that Dimmesdale was all the more aroused by the fact that Hester appeared inseduceable? Finally, was Dimmesdale seducing Hester merely to test the extent of his verbal powers and authority? Was it a mere game that got out of control?

Marshfield's relationship with Ms. Prynne is significant because she is what stimulates him and induces his recovery. As his reader, she tells him to write, much as Hester urges Dimmesdale to "Preach! Write! Act!" The relationship between reader and writer can be traced to Hawthorne's many prefaces, in which he openly proclaims this relationship:

> It had grown to be a custom with [the author of this romance], to introduce each of his humble publications with a familiar kind of Preface, addressed nominally to the Public at large, but really to a character with whom he felt entitled to use far greater freedom. He meant it for that one congenial friend—more comprehensive of his purposes, more appreciative of his success, more indulgent of his shortcomings, and, in all respects, closer and kinder than a brother—that all-sympathizing critic, in short, whom an author never actually meets, but to whom he implicitly makes his appeal, whenever he is conscious of having done his best.

Hawthorne goes on to state that he "never personally encountered" his reader, yet has maintained "a sturdy faith in his actual existence." However, he proceeds to say that in recent years he has experienced "a sad foreboding" that his reader is no longer "extant": "The Gentle Reader, in the case of any individual author, is apt to be extremely short-lived; he seldom outlasts a literary fashion, and, except in very rare instances, closes his weary eyes before the writer has half done with him."[16] With sadness, Hawthorne writes of the disappearance of "that unseen brother of the soul," and he remarks how he shall greatly miss his Reader's "apprehensive sympathy," which so encouraged him.

Marshfield's diary can be read as an allegory in which the writer is searching for and attempting to *know* his reader. As stated earlier, on one level Marshfield is hoping to seduce his flesh-and-blood reader, Ms. Prynne. Yet on another level, Marshfield could be fabricating everything, including the existence of Ms. Prynne. In the latter case, the novel demonstrates a writer's attempt literally to find his reader within the act of writing and then experience spiritual and physical communion with that reader. If read in this manner, the reader actually represents a part of the writer's self, and so the union between reader and writer can be viewed as the successful attempt on Marshfield's part to reintegrate his divided self. Much as Joseph Campbell sees all journeys as ones that reach deeper into the mind and unconscious, Marshfield's journey takes him into the depths of self in hopes of renewal.

From the outset, Marshfield is aware of the existence of a reader, whom he addresses as "gentle reader," "silent veiled reader," "you insatiable ideal reader," and so on. And as his writing accumulates, his interest in that reader grows. Conscious that "someone is reading these pages," Marshfield sets a trap of hairs and paper clips to verify, yet the reader fails to give him a sign. By the end of his third week he detects "an extra whiteness, as of erasure," on the previous day's page, and he makes out what he believes to be a word: "Can the word be 'Nice'? Ideal reader, can it be you? If the word was 'Nice,' why the naughty erasure, the negative second thought, the niggardly Indian-giving? But bless you, whoever you are, if you are, for this even so tentative intrusion into these pages' solipsism" (*MS*, 167). Continuing to speak to and ask questions of his reader, Marshfield becomes desperate for a sign. This desire for a sign, presumably from Ms. Prynne, becomes the central urgency of the novel and provides for a multilayered allegory (literary, re-

16. "Preface," *Marble Faun*, 1, 2.

ligious, sexual, psychological) in which the absent and impenetrable Ms. Prynne plays the multiple roles of reader, God, woman, and therapist.[17]

First, the literary level. As so aptly expressed by Hawthorne, a writer writes for "that one congenial friend," that "unseen brother of the soul," who is more indulgent, sympathetic, and intimate than a writer's reading public. With that reader in mind, the writer creates. At times he may even carry on an internal dialogue with that reader, ask questions of him, and seek advice. The writer's objective ultimately is to challenge, stimulate, and seduce that reader. This is precisely Marshfield's task in *A Month of Sundays*. Yet Marshfield carries the writer-reader relationship to the level of corporeality by seeking from his reader not only a sign but also, literally, physical contact. Claiming all along that he and Ms. Prynne have together made these pages, Marshfield realizes the appropriate final act is one of union or intercourse. In sexually overt language, Marshfield speaks as a writer of "entering" Ms. Prynne, and he speaks of her, his reader, as being "wet." As for the literary relationship between reader and writer, Marshfield has taken it as far as possible and written the appropriate conclusion to a grand allegory: "You have brought me to an edge, a slippery edge. And nothing left for me to do, dear Ideal Reader, but slip and topple off, gratefully" (*MS*, 228). Updike eroticizes the writer-reader relationship and demonstrates how language can arouse the flesh.

The second allegorical level relating to Marshfield's need for a sign concerns the religious. Both Dimmesdale and Marshfield are sensitive to and vigilant for signs from God. Dimmesdale interprets the falling meteor as a divine message addressed exclusively to himself, and he appears to fear and yet hope that God will strike him down with lightning for his sin. Typical of Updikean protagonists, Marshfield too looks to the physical and tangible for manifestations of the divine. Updike himself has stated that his family was inclined "to examine everything for God's fingerprints,"[18] and

17. The following critics have read *A Month of Sundays* as an allegory working on multiple levels: Robert Detweiler, *John Updike*, 146–51; Hunt, *Secret Things*, 181–94.

18. Updike, Interview with Jane Howard, "Can a Nice Novelist Finish First?," 76.

Marshfield echoes such scrutiny in displaying his own sensitivity to the appearance of the everyday physical world: "It was . . . in the *furniture* I awoke among . . . the moldings of the doorways and sashes of the windows . . . it was the carpets . . . that convinced me, that *told* me, God was, and was here. . . . Someone invisible had cared to make these things" (*MS*, 22–23). Yet Marshfield, whose first name is Thomas, is a doubter, a reluctant believer, and so he continues to be vigilant for some kind of revelation from God. Doubt so much colors his outlook that he states, "Even were the sky a neonated 3-D billboard flashing GOD EXISTS twenty-four hours a day we would contrive ways to doubt it" (*MS*, 213). And in a variety of diary entries, Marshfield describes himself looking through windows and at mirrors, waiting and watching. As a Barthian, believing that God is "Wholly Other" from humanity, perhaps Marshfield should not persist, yet he believes in revelation, and his ultimate desire is to see, experience, and be invaded by the divine—which in this case is Ms. Prynne. Like God she is the Other, a silent, absent, inaccessible presence. And Marshfield believes in her, has faith that she will come to him and minister unto his needs. Her ultimate arrival, the revelation of her giving herself to him, is the culminating religious allegory: Marshfield's reward for his faith and for his final preachable sermon. It also represents his personal sense of election and God's forgiveness. In *The Scarlet Letter* the narrator prophesies how an angel of revelation shall come, and in one respect Ms. Prynne is Marshfield's angel. Intercourse with her represents the union of the physical and spiritual in religion: Marshfield's spiritual faith in the Other is renewed, and he is resurrected both physically and spiritually with this final act.

The third allegorical level in the novel is the sexual, which is closely related to the religious. As Marshfield remarks of the women in his congregation, "how intuitively religious was their view of sex" (*MS*, 136). Updike himself has stated how *Couples* was "about sex as the emergent religion, as the only thing left." And de Rougemont has remarked how passionate love, or Eros, emerged as a reaction to Christianity and became a sort of Christian heresy.[19] The male quest for the "unattainable lady" parallels

19. Updike, "One Big Interview," 505; de Rougemont, *Love*, 74.

his quest for the unattainable God. The Other, whether it is God or woman, is what Marshfield searches for. Drawn by Ms. Prynne's "fascinating otherness," Marshfield believes his soul can only be fulfilled by meeting with her and admitting her into his spiritual and physical life. The sexual act that brings Marshfield and Ms. Prynne together differs, at least in Marshfield's estimation, from the previous sexual gymnastics that he engaged in with his female parishioners. Whereas those prior intimacies had more in common with Eros, this final act with Ms. Prynne is based on the more selfless love of agape. Marshfield had been insatiable and undirected while indulging in a selfish kind of love, but now, urged forth by Tillich, he sheds his solitary and desirous self for the love of oneself through loving one's neighbor. With Ms. Prynne, Marshfield gives freely instead of only taking. This act of coitus between the two of them is described as an act of mutual worship, not only of one another but also of God.

The fourth and final allegorical level relating to Marshfield's need for a sign concerns his therapy, and it is thus the psychological. Marshfield repeatedly alludes to the fact that his writing is a form of therapy. Not so unlike Philip Roth's *Portnoy's Complaint*, *A Month of Sundays* is a first-person confessional narrative, delivered by a man who has transgressed the boundaries of normal and acceptable social behavior. Both of these novels document exhaustive efforts by their narrators to explain and indulge themselves, and with the exception of a single line in each, the only voice we hear is that of the narrator himself. Interestingly enough, that single line in each signals a breakthrough in the mental state of the narrator: "So [*said the doctor*]. Now vee may perhaps to begin. Yes?";[20] "[*in pencil, in the slant hand of another:*] Yes—at last, a sermon that could be preached" (*MS*, 212). Placed near the end of their respective narratives, each indicates that success, however minor, has been achieved through therapy. In addition, the character delivering the single line happens to be the very character to whom the narrator directs his entire discourse. In *Portnoy's Complaint* that character is the "doctor" or psychoanalyst, and in *A Month of Sundays* it is Marshfield's "dear Reader." Each is a silent, almost absent presence, who listens and signals approval when

20. *Portnoy's Complaint*, 274.

progress has been achieved. The therapeutic taboo, of course, is against sexual relations between patient and therapist. And if we are to read the novel as a therapeutic allegory, Marshfield, the breaker of taboos, can be seen to have successfully seduced and penetrated that "other" who listens to him, his therapist.

A persistent question in *A Month of Sundays* is whether Marshfield's verbal self-therapy is successful: Has he written himself back to health? The question is made more complicated when attempting to understand what precisely constitutes "health." As Marshfield has already stated, he does not wish to return to the life he led prior to his adulterous revelation, that past life of "rote performance" and "daily grits." Yet to continue on his adulterous and irresponsible course also appears unacceptable. In order for Marshfield to progress, he must adopt some manner of thought that accommodates a compromise between free expression and social ethics.

Early in the novel, during his first sermon, Marshfield leans toward free expression, attempting to justify his adulterous behavior by milking the New Testament for tolerant responses to adultery; Marshfield thus strives to dissociate Christianity from proper social behavior. He bolsters his argument by citing the words, "Neither do I condemn thee," which is what Jesus says to the woman taken in adultery after none of her accusers has accepted His invitation to cast the first stone.[21] Searching through what he calls the most "domestic" of testaments, because it "sings of private hearths and intimate sorrows, not of palaces and battlefields," Marshfield discovers Jesus to be "abrasively liberal" upon matters of adultery and divorce (*MS*, 43, 45). He interprets the commandment "Be fruitful and multiply" as an encouragement to embrace adultery. And marriage, with its "token reverence, and wooden vows," ultimately fails to offer the spiritual and physical thrill of adultery:

> Wherein does the modern American man recover his sense of worth, not as dogged breadwinner and economic integer, but as romantic minister and phallic knight, as personage, embodiment, and hero? In adultery. . . . The adulterous man and woman arrive at the place of their tryst stripped of all the false uniforms society has assigned them; they come on no recommendation but their own, possess no creden-

21. John 8:11.

tials but those God has bestowed, that is, insatiable egos and work-able genitals.(*MS*, 46)

Though Marshfield in this early sermon rashly twists and manipulates biblical passages to promote a rejoicing in adultery, he nevertheless intelligently questions the relationship between social ethics and Christianity. As Updike himself has remarked in a statement that just as easily could have come from Marshfield: "People nowadays, at least liberal literary, assume that the Christian religion is primarily a system for enforcing ethics. It is not. It is an organization for distributing the good news of Jesus Christ."[22] For the Barthian in Marshfield, a vital belief in the Incarnation of Christ, not good ethical behavior, is central to Christianity. And in his first sermon he not only exposes this flaw in contemporary America's understanding of Christianity, but he also expresses his dissatisfaction with the institution of marriage, an existence that for him is spiritually and physically deathlike.

Marshfield, however, changes during his month in exile. His sermons increasingly become more acceptable to his demanding reader, Ms. Prynne, and his final exhortation is at last acknowledged as one that can be preached. Addressing his fellow ministers-in-exile in this sermon, Marshfield suggests that they should aspire not to the role of "romantic minister and phallic knight," but rather "to be visible and to provide men with the opportunity to profess the impossible that makes their lives possible" (*MS*, 210). They should be "steeples" rising above "man," and though they may crumble individually as men, they must continue to assume their priestly roles and offer hope and belief. Whereas Marshfield had earlier been unsure of his faith and of his ability to minister unto his flock, this final sermon is, in the words of Updike, a "reconfirmation of him in his vocation."[23] With renewed energy, faith, and confidence, he shall return to his role as Christian minister.

Marshfield's vocational transformation is paralleled in his theological transformation from Barth to Tillich. A longtime disciple of the neoorthodox Swiss, Marshfield once found a spiritual path in Barth: "Reading Barth gives me air I can breathe" (*MS*, 90). Yet as Ned Bork explains, Barth's theology leaves one with "this exul-

22. "Updike on Hawthorne," 3.
23. Letter to the author, January 26, 1989.

tant emptiness," which "panders to despair" and leads to isolation and passivity (*MS*, 90). By reading more Tillich, Marshfield becomes increasingly concerned with others. According to Updike, whereas Barth depreciates that which is human and sees an "absolute difference between human culture and God's revelation," Tillich interprets faith through culture. Tillich does not put God outside of nature and the world as Barth does, but he suggests that God is "present, [albeit] weakly, in everything." Hope thus resides in "love," which Tillich describes as "the urge for participation in the other one," and "the urge toward the reunion of the separated." Through his union with Ms. Prynne, Marshfield becomes whole again and is able to experience agape, which Tillich sees as "the self-transcendence of the religious element in love."[24] Through agape, Marshfield is able to shed his selfishness and reintegrate his divided self. It is also Tillich who was able to tolerate uncertainty, and who brought anxiety and doubt "into the sanctum, and called them holy emotions."[25]

Yet the ending of *A Month of Sundays* still poses problems. Though Marshfield gives evidence of a transformation—he appears sincere in reconfirming himself as a minister—how are we to deal with his final union with Ms. Prynne? Whether we interpret this scene literally or as an act of literary imagination, Marshfield's seduction and penetration of Ms. Prynne potentially signals a return to the adulterous behavior that landed him in Arizona to begin with. Has he or has he not made progress?

To better understand the ending of *A Month of Sundays* one should first consider the ending of *The Scarlet Letter*, particularly in regard to three essential points. First, Dimmesdale exits in a burst of energy and triumph. By confessing before the entire town with such dramatic intensity, he "dodges into death," enacting "a neat last revenge" upon Chillingworth (and perhaps even Hester). Michael Davitt Bell refers to the ending as Dimmesdale's success-

---

24. In his interview with Greiner, Updike remarks that "in the course of the book (it's been years since I wrote it, of course) I believe [Marshfield] was meant to change theologically, to become more Tillichian (deistic-humanist) than Barthian" ("Updike on Hawthorne," 3); Updike, "Tram Halt," 833, 836; Paul Tillich, *Morality and Beyond*, 40.
25. Updike, "Tram Halt," 836.

ful "staged *performance*."[26] Second, there is a good deal of ambiguity surrounding Dimmesdale's final moments. Did he actually confess? Was there indeed a "SCARLET LETTER . . . imprinted in the flesh" of his breast (*SL*, 258)? And third, Hester and Dimmesdale, the two lovers, remain separate, unable to unite. Though death finds them buried within one tomb, they are unable to come together spiritually and physically in life.

Updike's ending in *A Month of Sundays*, though radically different in tone and action than that of *The Scarlet Letter,* offers surprising parallels. Marshfield too ends with a successful "staged performance." Like Dimmesdale, he exits the novel triumphantly, ending in a burst of physical passion. Yet his physical passion leads to union and consummation between him and Ms. Prynne, not isolated death as is the case with Dimmesdale. Rejecting Hawthorne's tragic and perhaps prudish ending, Updike chooses to bring his lovers together in ecstatic union. The spiritual union that the two have already shared becomes fully realized when they come together physically. Whereas Dimmesdale cannot accept the promptings of the body, Marshfield realizes intense joy through the appetite of the flesh. By concluding the novel with the physical consummation, Updike is attempting to revise the moral and fleshly prudishness of Hawthorne's text. For Updike, matter is neither insignificant nor evil; it is as essential and as majestic as the spiritual.

Yet ambiguity persists in *A Month of Sundays*. Do Marshfield and Ms. Prynne actually have sex? And if so, how can one conclude that Marshfield has made any therapeutic progress during his month in exile? There are, of course, no easy answers; that is the point of intentional ambiguity. If we are, however, to assume that Marshfield and Ms. Prynne, as two flesh-and-blood characters, are engaged in sex, then are we not to conclude that Marshfield will return to his adulterous ways once back in society? Not necessarily. Known for his ambiguous endings, Updike is too subtle and too realistic to provide a false sense of closure, to maintain that Marshfield either will or will not indulge in fleshly desires with women other than his wife. Updike does not believe in clear resolution: "I feel that to be a person is to be in a situation of tension, is to be in a dialectical situation. A truly adjusted person is

26. "Arts of Deception," 49.

not a person at all—just an animal with clothes on."[27] Updike
then goes on to say that even with his happy endings there must be
a "but" at the end. Human attitudes are not as easily and clearly
resolved as some readers might wish or anticipate. Though Marshfield has apparently decided to return to his community and his
prior life—"I nod, weakly assenting. I am ready"—he nevertheless may continue, perhaps in a more subtle and less hostile manner, his personal rebellion (*MS*, 213). After all, one of the novel's
contentions is that adultery is not such an appalling human violation, that it can actually be spiritually invigorating and therapeutic. What the ending appears to maintain is that Marshfield,
during the course of his exile, has gained an understanding of his
earlier self-indulgence. And though he may not conform to social
prescription by becoming a faithful husband upon returning to
society, he has nonetheless been renewed in the desert, having
gained a greater sense of personal wholeness along with an appreciation for others.

Marshfield's quest is one that seeks reconciliation between matter and spirit, body and soul. In the course of his writing, he
locates the point of severance in the very founding of America: in
the crossing of the Atlantic, "baggage" was lost "having to do with
knowing, with acceptance of body by soul" (*MS*, 135). From its
Puritan heritage, America has castigated the body, forcing it to
become an evil stranger to its companion, the soul. Much like
Lawrence, who turned his gaze toward the American desert and
saw it as the place of hope, Marshfield strives in the Arizona desert
to repair the split and create a reconciled whole self in America.
He warns not to "castigate the body and its dark promptings," but
rather to become one with the body. And he argues that we know
things not only spiritually but also physically: "Transparency. My
unseeable theme. The way a golf swing reveals more of a man than
decades of mutual conversation" (*MS*, 190). Marshfield insists that
we must strive to understand the world physically if we are to
"move through it freely" and "empathize with God's work-
manship" (*MS*, 191). And his desire for Ms. Prynne's body signals
his desire to know her fully, and his hope that by knowing her they
may appear "a bit less opaque to one another."

27. "One Big Interview," 504.

The ending of *A Month of Sundays* is a first step in repairing the split found in American life between body and soul, as Marshfield and Ms. Prynne engage unselfishly in intercourse. Marshfield's final words—"I pray my own face, a stranger to me, saluted in turn"—inform us that his inner self, much as in the initial diary entry, is still and will always to some degree be dislocated from his outer self. Yet in his attempt to reconcile and reconsider who he is, Marshfield moves to a new appreciation of his "neighbor." From the solitude and masturbation of his early writing, he arrives at mutually pleasurable intercourse and a newly aroused feeling for community. Unlike the frail Dimmesdale, who withers and dies, Marshfield recovers and realizes a reconfirmation of himself in his vocation. Through language, Marshfield writes himself out of his predicament and back into the world of others.

TWO

Roger's Version
Eyes with a Strange
Penetrating Power

I f *The Scarlet Letter* from Dimmesdale's perspective is a discourse on verbalization, then from Chillingworth's perspective it is a discourse on visualization. Chillingworth is first seen in the chapter entitled "The Recognition," in which he and Hester, after a long absence, visually recognize one another at the marketplace: "The stranger had bent his eyes on Hester Prynne. It was carelessly, at first, like a man chiefly accustomed to look inward. . . . Very soon, however, his look became keen and penetrative. . . . When he found the eyes of Hester Prynne fastened on his own, and saw that she appeared to recognize him, he slowly and calmly raised his finger, made a gesture with it in the air, and laid it on his lips" (*SL*, 61). We soon realize that this stranger, who possesses a "slight deformity of the figure," is the very "misshapen scholar" upon whom Hester had earlier reflected. And in that reflection Hester contemplated Chillingworth in regard to his optical powers: "She beheld . . . a pale, thin, scholar-like visage, with eyes dim and bleared by the lamp-light that had served them to pore over many ponderous books. Yet those same bleared optics had a strange, penetrating power, when it was their owner's purpose to read the human soul" (*SL*, 58). As a man of "remarkable intelligence" who has given his best years "to feed the hungry dream of knowledge," Chillingworth relies almost solely upon his eyes (not his mouth, like Dimmesdale), which have allowed him to seek out "truth in books." Yet he is more than a mere "bookworm" who can proficiently scan pages of typographical print. His visual abilities are such that he can see beyond the physical and phenomenal world into the inner sanctum of the soul. As he explains to Hester, he possesses a "sympathy" that makes him adept at reading the souls of others.

Vowing to solve the riddle of Pearl's paternity and deliver the mystery into the light of day, Chillingworth directs his vision toward the minister's interior world, such that "the very inmost soul of the latter seemed to be brought out before his eyes" (*SL,* 140). Through his superior vision, Chillingworth is able to locate and prey upon Dimmesdale's inner vulnerabilities so as to torture him. Revenge, of course, is the impetus for Chillingworth's visual penetration of the minister's soul; however, a surprising intimacy soon develops between the men in which they experience "with a tremulous enjoyment . . . the occasional relief of looking at the universe through the medium of another kind of intellect" (*SL,* 123). By means of his optical powers, which allow him to become "not a spectator only, but a chief actor, in the poor minister's interior world," Chillingworth comes to find that his closest physical and emotional bond is with Dimmesdale (*SL,* 140).

The significance of visualization in *The Scarlet Letter* extends beyond the character of Chillingworth. In the opening chapters, Hester stands before the staring townspeople as an example and as "the object of severe and universal observation" (*SL,* 60). And during the course of the novel she and her badge of shame continue to attract the eyes of others:

> Another peculiar torture was felt in the gaze of a new eye. When strangers looked curiously at the scarlet letter,—and none ever failed to do so,—they branded it afresh into Hester's soul. . . . But then, again, an accustomed eye had likewise its own anguish to inflict. Its cool stare of familiarity was intolerable. From first to last, in short, Hester Prynne had always this dreadful agony in feeling a human eye upon the token. (*SL,* 85–86)

Hester's scarlet *A,* as Richard Brodhead points out, "is almost always before us."[1] Whether displayed on Hester's breast, or reflected in suits of armor, pools, or brooks, the scarlet *A* is the focal point of the novel. And it is the task of the reader to observe the enigmatic letter in order to understand its meaning and value.

---

1. *Hawthorne, Melville, and the Novel,* 54.

In addition, Roy Male describes how many of the novel's chapter titles spring from an effort to gain a better perspective, and how Hawthorne utilizes a vocabulary that emphasizes vision: *scene, eye, witness, interview, spectacle, perspective, speculation, spectator*.[2] Many of the novel's key scenes—Chillingworth eyeing the bare bosom of the sleeping Dimmesdale, Dimmesdale witnessing the streaking meteor, the three scaffold scenes—highlight the act of seeing and point to the difficulties in seeing clearly and accurately. Events and symbols in *The Scarlet Letter* are notoriously ambiguous and enigmatic, and the act of seeing varies according to perspective, lighting, optical powers, and the nature of the particular object being viewed. One could even look beyond *The Scarlet Letter* to see how the significance of visualization is apparent in so much of Hawthorne's other work, including *The American Notebooks, The Blithedale Romance*, "Sights from a Steeple," and "Rappaccini's Daughter." Hawthorne's protagonists are continually climbing hills, peeking through windows and curtains, and ascending towers and churches to gain a better perspective.

Hawthorne's interest in visualization is not lost upon Updike, who appropriates the function of seeing as his central metaphor in *Roger's Version*, the most successful novel in the trilogy and perhaps the most significant novel to date in Updike's oeuvre. Roger Lambert, a divinity school professor at what appears to be Harvard, takes his first name from Hawthorne's physician and his last apparently from the eighteenth-century German physicist Johann Heinrich Lambert. Among his many contributions to science, the historical Lambert was responsible for a variety of innovations in the study of light, and the "lambert," a measure of light intensity, was named in his honor. Updike's Lambert, though rather staid, conservative, and "tweedy" on the surface, burns inside with a brightness and luminosity that inspire his tremendous vision: "Since the age of eight, when I was praised by the family ophthalmologist for prattling off even the bottom line of his chart, I have taken an innocent pride in the keenness of my eyesight" (*RV*, 17). Yet, as with Chillingworth, Roger Lambert's superior vision transcends the purely physical and has more to do with his ability to see into the hearts and minds of others than with his ability to read an eye chart. Like

2. *Hawthorne's Tragic Vision*, 101.

Chillingworth, Lambert delights in seeing into the interior selves of others, and also in seeing the exterior world through the eyes of others. Such optical versatility exhilarates and empowers him.

As a narrator and observer, Roger endeavors to fine-tune his narrative elements by being most attentive to the changing conditions in light and perspective.[3] Largely an outsider and spectator, Roger knows the world not through emotional involvement or palpability, but through watching. In virtually every scene in the novel we are made aware of the type of light that is being generated: "gray autumnal light," "double-barrelled light," "hospital light," "islands of light in a jagged arboreal ocean," "fluorescent lights." We are also alerted to the direction from which the light arrives: "behind me," "overhead," "from underneath," "at my back." Light is invariably changing, transforming those objects and people with which it comes in contact, and no one is more aware of this than Roger: "[Dale's] easy tallness, which in the slant chapel light of my office he quickly folded into the university chair opposite my desk, here in my front hall loomed, all suited and combed, as a costume of grace, a form of potency" (*RV*, 95). In *Roger's Version* light may often intensify and expose some hidden feature, much as light from the meteor in *The Scarlet Letter* "kindled up the sky" and made "vivid" the fiendish expression of Roger Chillingworth's face.

Roger also makes a habit of carefully observing the eyes of others, particularly in regard to how light transforms those eyes: Esther's eyes were "like my recent visitor's, awash with window light, though their blue favored the green end of the spectrum and my young visitor's the gray. My own eyes, to complete the chart, are a somewhat melting chocolate, a dark wet bearish brown that makes me look, according to the susceptibilities of the witness, angry or about to cry" (*RV*, 45). Moments later Roger adjusts his description, making note of Esther's "green, hyperthyroid eyes,"

3. In a preface to *Roger's Version*, Updike states that

in shaping this story with [Roger Chillingworth] . . . I have done more adjusting and fine-tuning than, if memory serves, for any other novel. Regulating the recurrence of adjectives and tinkering with the eye and hair color of characters, numbering the incarnations of Pearl, meshing theology with pornography and fitting the segments of my imaginary city together, I felt at times like one of the mechanics hopelessly engaged on Charles Babbage's Analytical Engine, the first computer. ("A 'Special Message' [*Roger's Version*]," 858) and in the course of the novel her green eyes are observed with ever so slight distinctions: "Her bulging eyes were very green in the light from the front door"; "The hungry green of her eyes with their gentle hyperthyroid bulge"; "Her eyes have been flushed a richer, kinder green by her orgasm"; "She appraised me with her pale green eyes" (*RV*, 96, 126, 157, 329).

Esther is not the only character whose eyes are carefully observed by Roger. Verna's eyes vary from "light brown" to "amber" to "pink," and her daughter Paula's eyes range from blue to brown: "Her eyes, which had once looked navy-blue to me, had become brown, shades deeper than Verna's" (*RV*, 222). That eye color is subject to change is hardly startling. What is interesting though is Roger Lambert's propensity to read the eyes of others, which can best be explained by his own statement: "The eye is the soul's window, and we atavistically trust its information to be complete" (*RV*, 233). By looking at and through the eyes of others, Roger is endeavoring to penetrate into their souls, where he can not only know their world but also control and modulate it.

As shall become apparent, visualization serves as a metaphor on multiple levels in *Roger's Version*. Roger Lambert is obsessed with visually following the movements of Dale Kohler and attempting to imagine the world as it would appear through Dale's eyes. By secretly observing Dale's life, and by seeing through his eyes, the aging and depressed Roger is stimulated and nourished. Dale Kohler is equally obsessed with vision as his project entails his attempt literally to see God, to wait for His image to appear like a revelation on the computer screen. Also, there are various discussions in the novel about scientists and scientific theories that have attempted "to see" or visually imagine: the moment of Creation; the smallest particle in existence, the quark, which functions as the essential building block of the world; and the cosmological limits of the universe. Finally, Roger endeavors to see Boston from every possible angle and perspective, which relates not only to Dale's undertaking on the computer (to re-create the visual world from myriad angles and perspectives) and to Updike's task as a novelist (to see Roger's world and re-create it on paper), but also to Hawthorne's attempt, particularly in *The American Notebooks* and "Sights from a Steeple," to see the city of Boston from various points of observation.

In appropriating visualization as his central metaphor in *Roger's*

Version, Updike reminds us of the significance of vision in *The Scarlet Letter* and of the difficulty of envisioning anything accurately and fully. Yet Updike expands upon the work of Hawthorne. First, Updike liberates vision from Christian ethics, allowing the reader to see that to which Hawthorne only alludes. Whereas in Hawthorne's novel a visual description of the moment of consummation between Dimmesdale and Hester is avoided, Updike's Lambert concentrates upon this scene, visually re-creating it for self-stimulation. For Roger the act of seeing is a creative sexual stimulant, and he endeavors to see everything, particularly the activities of the flesh. Second, in *Roger's Version* Updike is attempting to undo the traditional body-soul division in which "matter verges upon being evil" and "matter and spirit are inevitably at war."[4] Following Tertullian and Barth, Updike's Roger Lambert argues for the significance of corporeality, blasting those "who make an outcry against the flesh . . . who accuse it of being unclean . . . infirm, guilty . . . burdensome, troublesome" (*RV*, 152). "The flesh is man," Lambert declares, and the activities of the flesh must not be repressed. Vigorously affirming corporeal impulse, Updike utilizes vision as a vehicle for understanding how flesh and spirit work together: Dale endeavors through the vision of a computer to bring God the spirit into the flesh, and Roger's visual fantasies have a stimulatory effect upon his flesh. Finally, *Roger's Version* demonstrates how modern technology and knowledge have increased the human possibilities for vision. In a novel focused upon our visual ability to perceive and digest information, the computer, as we shall see through Dale Kohler's project, offers a new mode of vision.

Roger's Version begins with Roger recalling his initial appointment with Dale Kohler, a computer-science graduate student in search of a research grant. Characterizing his life as comfortable, handsome, uneventful, and rather safe, Roger finds in Dale "something challenging, something of impudence and insinuation" (*RV*, 5). Dressed in his academic tweed, Roger has tried to resist any type of passionate engagement with others, preferring to insulate and isolate himself. Yet there is something in Dale's youthful en-

4. Updike, "Hawthorne's Creed," 77.

thusiasm that triggers and upsets the soothing comfort of Roger's world. To begin with, Dale is a native of Akron and thus a "fellow Buckeye." Having come to the East to escape the "muggy, suffocating heartland," Roger finds Dale to be a reminder of that "dismal and forsaken" life that he left back in his native Cleveland. In *Roger's Version*, Boston and the East remain a veritable New World, luring those from the prohibitions and complacent mediocrity of the heartland toward a greater spiritual and physical freedom. As Chillingworth and Dimmesdale issued from a Stuart-controlled England and sailed west for the free shores of New England, Lambert and Kohler have issued from Ohio and traveled east to the sophisticated and culturally diverse city of Boston. More than three hundred years since its founding, Boston remains a hub, drawing people within its bounds and literally "sucking village and farmland into its orbit" (*RV*, 317). As Updike explains in a preface, this is his attempt at a "city novel," and as will become apparent, *Roger's Version* is very much about America as big city, and America as Boston.[5]

In appearance, Dale Kohler resembles Arthur Dimmesdale: young, tall, and rather pale. Roger, who most obviously resents and envies Dale's youth, takes a dislike to the young man's "waxy pallor" and feels intimidated by his height. Serving as an allusion to *The Scarlet Letter*, in which Chillingworth is described as "small in stature," Roger Lambert proves to be most sensitive to those who are taller than he, and in turn he experiences a sensation of power and control over those who are smaller. The concern with height points to Roger's obsession with the human physique; he continually seeks to understand his relation to others as reflected in the literal texture, weight, and height of their respective human flesh. Height also plays a significant role in visualization; a person of greater height is afforded a higher vista, a more advantageous perspective.

The taller Dale Kohler is also passionately pious. Possessing a born-again Christian's zeal for prayer and biblical quotation, Dale hopes to use his knowledge of computers and science literally to find God, to *see* Him appear on a computer screen. Taking his first name (along with his piety) from Hawthorne's minister, Dale ap-

---

5. "A 'Special Message' [*Roger's Version*]," 856.

parently takes his last from Kaufmann Kohler, one of the most influential theologians of Reform Judaism in America. Rabbi Kohler's quest for the reconciliation of traditional faith with modern knowledge is one shared by Dale Kohler. Incidentally, Rabbi Kohler also spent a good deal of time in the Midwest, and in particular in Ohio. Finally, the surname Kohler may additionally refer to the plumbing manufacturer, which is appropriate considering that Dale wishes to tinker with the plumbing of the universe.

In a succession of meetings with Roger, Dale outlines his project as follows: Too many coincidences and perfect mathematical figures obtain in charting how the universe was created. The odds that it happened as it did by chance are astronomically low, and so he concludes that "there's no intrinsic reason for those constants to be what they are except to say *God made them that way*" (*RV*, 14). Imagining God to be that "purposeful Intelligence" who "fine-tuned the physical constants and the initial conditions," Dale, in his research proposal, determines "*to demonstrate from existing physical and biological data, through the use of models and manipulations on the electronic digital computer, the existence of God, i.e., of a purposive and determining intelligence behind all phenomena*" (*RV*, 75–76). In a novel about visualization, Dale is determined to see that which is unseeable, shine a light on that which has no understandable physical essence. He is resolved to demonstrate that "God is *breaking through*," and that "God's face is staring right out at us" (*RV*, 20). "God can't hide any more," Dale declares, expressing his hope that he can demonstrate to the people of the world, who have been intimidated into not believing in God by the atheistic scientific community, that the existence of God can be proven. If successful, the pious and born-again Dale would no doubt become the savior of humanity.

Roger Lambert, Updike's recurring Barthian who envisions God as "Wholly Other," finds Dale's project "aesthetically and ethically repulsive. Aesthetically because it describes a God Who lets Himself be intellectually trapped, and ethically because it eliminates faith from religion" (*RV*, 24). Contending that God can only be placed "totally on the other side of the humanly understandable," Roger views Dale's project as egotistical and blasphemous. Answering Dale's passionate pursuit of God with his own "patronizing but often urgent defense of God's privacy," Roger sees himself as "the heavy hand of the Church suppressing youthful enthusiasms."[6] The professor of Christian heresy, who occasionally aspires to the role of social heretic himself (like Tertullian, whom he is so fond of quoting), moves to squelch an attempted heresy: Dale's technological pursuit of God. Ultimately the situation becomes rather ironic: the scientist is obsessed with proving God's existence, while the theologian adamantly "rejects the possibility of such a proof."[7]

Dale resembles the scientists found in Hawthorne, such as Rappaccini and Aylmer (of "The Birth-mark"), who, as Hawthorne writes in "The Hall of Fantasy," "had gotten possession of some crystal fragment of truth, the brightness of which so dazzled them that they could see nothing else in the wide universe." Updike refers to these scientists as "ill-fated disrupters of the universal balance," and he casts Dale Kohler in their likeness.[8] Like Hawthorne's scientists, Dale utilizes his knowledge to push the limits of nature and expand his power. And even though Dale initially appears to represent Lawrence's version of a whole and unified self, one in which religion and science have become reconciled, his quest is excessive and self-important, and like Hawthorne's scientists, he is doomed to fail.

What emerges as the central conflict in the novel is the intellectual, spiritual, and physical battle waged between Roger and Dale.[9] Subscribing to Lawrence's reading of *The Scarlet Letter*, Updike casts Roger as "the old male authority" who is locked in a struggle for intellectual superiority with Dale, the "new spiritual aspirer." According to Lawrence, Chillingworth "hates the new spiritual aspirers . . . with a black, crippled hate," and it becomes his raison d'être to bring on the downfall of "the spiritual saint."[10] Updike utilizes a vocabulary that is appropriate to battle. Dale had come at Roger with his "drawn sword of youth," and Roger defends

6. Morey, "Sexual Language," 1036; Eder, "Roger's Version," 3.
7. Eder, "Roger's Version," 3.
8. Hawthorne, "The Hall of Fantasy," *Mosses from an Old Manse*, 180; Updike, "Hawthorne's Creed," 78.
9. For a related discussion of how the metaphor of "wrestling" operates in *Roger's Version*, see John N. Duvall's excellent article "The Pleasure of Textual/Sexual Wrestling: Pornography and Heresy in *Roger's Version*."
10. *Studies*, 105.

himself with his "armor of amiable tweed," eventually becoming "captive" to Dale's "milky effrontery" and "assaultive verbalizing earnestness." At one point Roger realizes that "it would take more of an attack than I could mount to shake him" (*RV*, 15). And in attempting to subdue the "predatory" Dale, who has a knack for finding "the soft and tender spots of [Roger's] enamel," Roger resorts to the subtle and manipulative tactics of "predator satiation," in which he adopts a "non-combative" tone and allows Dale to "argue himself into exhaustion" (*RV*, 81, 171).

Yet Roger's feelings for Dale are not entirely hateful and combative. Studying his opponent in his office, Roger lists his sentiments for Dale as "physical repugnance, at his waxiness . . . loathing of his theories . . . envy of his faith and foolish hope . . . a certain attraction . . . a grateful inkling that he was injecting a new element into my life . . . an odd and sinister empathy: he kept inviting my mind out of its tracks to follow him on his own paths through the city" (*RV*, 89–90). As Hawthorne remarks in the conclusion to *The Scarlet Letter*, "It is a curious subject of observation and inquiry, whether hatred and love be not the same thing at bottom. Each, in its utmost development, supposes a high degree of intimacy and heart-knowledge; each renders one individual dependent for the food of his affections and spiritual life upon another; each leaves the passionate lover, or the no less passionate hater, forlorn and desolate by the withdrawal of his object" (*SL*, 260). In the relationships between Chillingworth and Dimmesdale, and Lambert and Kohler, there exists an intense degree of attachment, which borders upon the homoerotic. However, it is only through the configuration of the adulterous triangle, in which a woman (Hester, Esther, Verna) stands as the supposed object of affection, that these heterosexual male characters are able to express their homoerotic tendencies. Unlike any other work in Updike's predominantly heterosexual oeuvre, *Roger's Version* concentrates on a relationship between two men.

It is at the close of Roger's first meeting with Dale that perhaps the most interesting aspect of *Roger's Version* arises. As Roger notices Dale's eyes wandering toward the wall of books, a spiritual transaction takes place in which Roger imagines the two of them as "shards of shattered Godhead captive in the darks of matter. . . . We seemed to float, Dale and I, in lightly etched immensities of space" (*RV*, 26–27). Roger is then "disconcerted by a strange un-willed vision," in which his "disembodied mind empathetically" follows Dale down the hall and out of the divinity school. Thus begins a series of visions, fantasies, and daydreams on Roger's part, in which his mind travels through space and follows the physical and mental movements of Dale Kohler. Walking home from school several hours later, Roger has "the sensation of following in [Dale's] steps," and he imagines Dale having noticed a "strange emblematic leaf three hours earlier" (*RV*, 29, 30–31). Not only does Roger's reading of the pink sugar-maple leaf allude to the reading of the meteor and to the scarlet *A* itself in Hawthorne's novel, but it also points to Updike's belief that the physical world can be read for spiritual signs.

In following Dale, Roger is able to escape his otherwise stale and predictable existence, living vicariously through the youthful graduate student. Here Updike follows Hawthorne and James, who shared as their "deepest bond" a "sense of literature's essential vicariousness." According to Brodhead, both Hawthorne and James "know the need imaginative creation appeals to as the need (in Miles Coverdale's words) 'to live in other lives': the need to remedy a felt life-deficiency not by living one's own life fully but by appropriating life in simulated or surrogate forms."[11] By groping his way into Dale's reality, Roger is able to absorb and feed upon the life of another while escaping the dullness of his own being. It is not until *The Witches of Eastwick* (1984) and *Roger's Version* (1986) that vicariousness surfaces as a significant feature in Updike's fiction, and Hawthorne appears to be the primary influence behind this new aspect in Updike's writing.

In sharing Dale's "field of vision," Roger is literally able to see anew. When he imagines seeing his wife Esther through the eyes of Dale, she becomes transformed spiritually and physically: "I saw her through his eyes, my little wife, her tense and tidy figure fore-shortened even more from his angle than from mine. . . . Esther had put on a glint, an alertness, an older woman's assured and ironic potential playfulness" (*RV*, 96). Through Dale's eyes Roger rediscovers his wife and experiences a renewed sexual interest in her: "I saw her close up, through Dale's eyes . . . and I felt a sexual

11. *School of Hawthorne*, 183.

stir in my lap" (*RV,* 126). Though the novel centers upon the struggle between Roger and Dale, with Esther serving as a secondary character whom Roger modulates in order to penetrate more deeply into Dale's life, it is equally feasible to read the novel as a struggle between Roger and Esther, in which Dale is used as a pawn by the Lamberts in an effort to revitalize their marriage. Updike is forcing us to reconsider the dynamics of the *Scarlet Letter* triangle: Is the relationship between Chillingworth and Dimmesdale the primary attachment in the novel, or, as Lawrence suggests, are Chillingworth and Hester accomplices of sorts, attempting to ruin the pure spiritual man?

In *Roger's Version*, Updike creates a variety of possible triangular configurations, which can partially be explained through the discussions of particle physics and binary number systems that appear in the novel. Regarding the former, Updike turns his attention not only to seeing the largest thing in the universe, God, but also to seeing the smallest, the quark (which takes its name from Joyce's *Finnegans Wake:* "Three quarks for Muster mark").[12] Though a quark, like God, has never actually been seen, it serves for the time being as the smallest fundamental particle and the essential building block of matter, and it provides a way of understanding nature in its bare simplicity. Theories concerning the quark (and the basic dynamics of particle physics) have had a tremendous influence upon science's understanding of the origin and evolution of the universe, and Myron Kriegman, Roger Lambert's neighbor, helps us to understand how the quark resembles the adulterous triangle in terms of structure and dynamics. Also, since the quark is the fundamental particle of matter from which we all are made, it makes perfect sense, as Updike metaphorically suggests, that human beings respond to some of the same principles of dynamics that affect the quark.

Much like the characters in Updike's novels of adultery, quarks do not exist in isolation but in combination with other quarks; generally three quarks form a neutron or proton, or what some physicists refer to as a "particle family."[13] As Kriegman explains in the course of his predatory feeding upon Dale and his theories,

---

12. Joyce is quoted in James S. Trefil, *From Atoms to Quarks,* 138.
13. Trefil, *From Atoms to Quarks,* 138.

"[quarks] invariably occur in threes, and cannot be pried apart" (*RV*, 301). In bonding, quarks form "a *knot*, a knot that tightens on itself and won't pull apart," and it is its triadic nature, Kriegman argues, that holds it together: "You can't make a knot in two dimensions because there's no over or under, and—here's the fascinating thing, see if you can picture it—you can make a ravelling in four dimensions but it isn't a knot, it won't hold, it will just pull apart, it won't per*sist*" (*RV*, 302). In *Roger's Version*, knots of three predominate as the primary social structure bonding characters together, and multiple adulterous triangles are formed in the novel: 1. Roger, his first wife, Lillian, and his then mistress, Esther; 2. Roger, his second wife, Esther, and Dale Kohler; 3. Roger, Esther, and Verna Ekelof; 4. Roger, Verna, and Dale; 5. Dale, Esther, and Verna; 6. Roger, Verna, and Roger's half-sister, Edna; 7. Roger's father, Roger's mother Alma, and Roger's stepmother Veronica. And other triangles, nonadulterous in nature, are also formed: 1. Roger, Esther, and their son, Richie; 2. Roger, Verna, and her daughter, Paula; 3. Roger, Esther, and Paula; 4. Dale, Esther, and Richie; 5. Esther, Dale, and their unborn fetus; 6. Roger, Edna, and their father. The possibilities are endless as Updike fiddles with and manipulates the configurations of his triangles, revealing in their composition a greater sense of dynamics than that found in relationships that operate between just two people. Updike is inclined to place his characters in triadic bonds, and he demonstrates how individuals often relate to one another and interact with others through the agency of a third party.

One should also note that quarks, like human beings, carry an electric charge and undergo strong forces of attraction and repulsion; Roger remarks how at one point Esther "triggered in me that old enchantment, that fourteen-year-old sense of the space in her vicinity being sacred, charged with electrons agitating to one's own" (*RV*, 50). There exists an electric dynamics between quarks such that if a quark attempts to leave a proton it feels itself being pulled back more strongly, much as Dale Kohler (according to Roger) feels himself being drawn back into the triangle with Roger and Esther. Quarks may also alter their spin and even their identity, disturbing the composition of the triadic union of which they are a part; as we see in *Roger's Version*, the dynamics of the various triangular configurations is always changing. Quarks may also penetrate one another and exchange energy and identity in the process. Finally, it is possible to have a quark family in which one quark orbits around the other two. Such a model helps to visualize how Roger, as narrator and modulator, functions in his triangular relationships; as the orbiting quark, Roger continually surrounds and observes the actions of others.[14]

The binary number system, which functions as the mathematical basis for digital computer operations, also serves as a metaphor for understanding relationships in *Roger's Version*. In the binary number system, figures are represented as being in one of two states: open or closed, hot or cold, on or off. Explaining how a computer is made up of just switches and gates that move current around, Dale demonstrates that with three switches (OR, AND, and NOT), a "complexity of ins and outs," ons and offs, can be created: "You can run these same two four-bit numbers into AND gates along with their own inverses, produced in these NOTS here, and then take those two outputs through an OR; what the output tells you, oh one one oh, is where the original inputs agreed: it's cold where they did and hot where they didn't" (*RV*, 111–12). As Judie Newman points out, "the erotic permutations of the quartet [Roger, Esther, Dale, Verna] are anticipated in binary and computer imagery."[15] As the pairs within the quartet form and re-form, they produce various currents, and the adjectives *hot* and *cold*, while accurate computer terminology, relate perfectly to the sexual nature of the pairings. Updike succeeds in demonstrating how vastly different systems—binary number operations, particle physics, adulterous triangle configurations—share principles of dynamics and help to explain the workings of one another.

As mentioned above, Roger Lambert is involved in a variety of triadic relationships, some of which are sexual in nature. Fourteen years previous, when married to Lillian and employed as a minister in a town in upstate New York, Roger and Esther played the roles of Dimmesdale and Hester, scandalizing the parish with their adultery. It had been a time of "decided pleasure," in which Roger found it rather "sweet" to affront public opinion: "We were like

14. For an extended discussion of quarks, see Trefil's works *From Atoms to Quarks*, 131–90, and *The Moment of Creation*, 64–69, 115–18.
15. *John Updike*, 149.

two gladiators whose heated grappling fascinates an entire arena" (*RV*, 103). (At an earlier point in the novel Roger again appears like Dimmesdale, recalling his past self as "a young man who thought that here [in the pages of Karl Barth], definitively and forever, he had found the path, the voice, the style, and the method to save within himself and to present to others the Christian faith" [*RV*, 40].) What is most interesting about Roger having once played the role of Dimmesdale is the implicit suggestion that Chillingworth/Lambert functions as the older version of Dimmesdale/Kohler. In other words, Dimmesdales, if they live long enough, become Chillingworths. It is apparent that there are tremendous similarities between the two men in *The Scarlet Letter*—their obsessiveness and need for privacy, their bookishness and interest in Hester—and on one level Roger's attraction to Dale can be read as his desire for his younger self. Through the flexibility of his triangular configurations, in which a character may temporarily come to play all three roles, Updike not only demonstrates the existing similarities between Chillingworth, Dimmesdale, and Hester, but he also reveals how they operate as three perspectives on or aspects of a single consciousness.

In the years since their adulterous scandal, Roger and Esther have "slipped into conformity"; their sex life has dwindled and they have become smothered by boredom (perhaps this would have happened to Hester and Dimmesdale had they gone off to Europe together). In the stasis of marriage, Roger feels Esther's "boredom pulling at me, sucking at me," and he resists by turning to a third party and, in effect, becoming the Chillingworth figure, the manipulator. The heated young minister who once turned to adultery for rejuvenation becomes, through marriage and aging, the curmudgeon who must now resort to voyeurism, manipulation, and vicariously experienced adultery for renewal. And in his new role as Chillingworth, Roger attempts to rekindle the passion of his marriage to Esther; as he states, "Cathexis is . . . never lost, just mislaid" (*RV*, 50). Through the youthful vitality of third parties, in this case Dale Kohler and Verna Ekelof, Roger attempts to revive his marriage.

The central triangle in the novel is of course that of Roger, Dale, and Esther, and if we are to adopt Lawrence's reading of *The Scarlet Letter*, Dale serves as the pawn that the Lamberts utilize to improve their conjugality. Through Dale, each attempts to annoy, hurt, reawaken, and anger the other. When Roger first mentions Dale, describing him as a rather pushy and obnoxious "science type," Esther immediately sides with Dale, stating that "he sounds like a rather touching young man." According to Roger, she is "siding with this unknown youth only in order to annoy me" (*RV*, 43). Thus, he imagines her not to be in love with the younger man, but rather to be using Dale to annoy him and to indulge her own selfish pleasures. If we are to believe Roger, it is as if he and his wife wage their domestic battles through the body and soul of Dale: "Dale has sensed, at times, that his mistress's passionate contortions have something in them of exhibitionistic defiance, of 'showing' an invisible third party, of effecting a balance involving factors that preceded his arrival on her scene" (*RV*, 239–40). Esther renders Dale dependent and vulnerable, and although she asks him to rescue her from her marriage, her plea is a cruel tease considering that she is so "securely attached to the social role and domestic furniture that come with her wifery" to Roger (*RV*, 239). And of Esther's motives, Verna remarks that "[It's] like she *wanted* to drive [Dale] crazy" (*RV*, 319). There is a cruelty to Esther's actions, and Dale has been the victim; however, one must be reminded of the fact that all of this emanates from Roger's perspective. When Dale speaks, it is Roger placing words in his mouth, and when Dale and Esther engage in sexual acrobatics, it is Roger who sees and describes the action. Roger's narrative, like Marshfield's in *A Month of Sundays*, is unreliable. As Roger himself admits, "There are great glutinous holes in my recollection of our conversation" (*RV*, 116). Furthermore, Roger obviously could not know the dialogue between Esther and Dale when they were tucked away in naked intimacy in the Malvin Lane attic, nor could he know the series of events that transpired during Dale's exhaustive nightly vigil in front of the computer screen in the fortress-like Cube. One must continually question Roger's perceptions and motives.

In *Roger's Version* the Hester prefiguration is fragmented such that the role is played by both Esther Lambert and Verna Ekelof. A well-to-do housewife, Esther is Roger's second wife, and like Hester, she is a good deal younger than her husband (fourteen years in this case). Like her ancestral sister, Esther is an angel of mercy,

working part-time for little pay at a nearby day-care center (is Updike suggesting that the saintly Hester operates as a mythical predecessor for contemporary females who turn to volunteer work or
work for little pay?). And like Hester, Esther finds an outlet for her
more untamed emotions in art; Hester's needlepoint is matched by
Esther's "slashing, angular, gobby" paintings, what Roger calls
her "big angry abstractions." Both women have also encountered
community censure (Esther broke up Roger's first marriage when
he, in his Dimmesdale role, was a minister in a small town); both
have experienced loneliness and boredom; and both attempt to escape their foundering marriages through adultery. The most no-
ticeable difference between Hester and Esther concerns their
physical appearance. Unlike Hester, who is tall and robust with
dark hair, Esther is a tiny woman with a "thin petite figure and
fluffy upswept head of gingery red hair" (RV, 33). Compulsive
about maintaining her one-hundred-pound weight, Esther is perhaps America's idea of fitness and beauty during the Reagan
administration, continuing the evolution charted by Hawthorne
in *The Scarlet Letter:* "Throughout that chain of ancestry, every
successive mother has transmitted to her child a fainter bloom, a
more delicate and briefer beauty, and a slighter physical frame, if
not a character of less force and solidity, than her own" (SL, 50).
Esther Lambert continues that chain, adopting the rather contemporary attitude of "the thinner the better"; with Esther,
Puritan privation continues.

Despite the similarities, Esther, at least initially, does not re-
mind one of Hester. Hester is an attractive, sensuous woman who
gains our respect and interest; Esther is a skinny boozer, prone to
snide remarks, cynicism, and yawning boredom. Two approaches
help to explain. First, Updike is a realist; there are no saints in his
novels. Though many readers have elevated Hester to the position
of early feminist saint, Updike resists, seeking instead to highlight
the darker and more vengeful side of Hawthorne's heroine, as set
down by Lawrence (more on this in Chapter 3). And second, one
must constantly be alert to the fact that the narrative comes from
the perspective of Roger. A different narrator might have chosen to
emphasize Esther's more redeemable qualities; she is, after all, a
good mother, a community volunteer, and a sensitive lover. Yet in
the eyes of Roger, irritated at her for her adultery and their dwin-

dling marriage, she becomes hardened. Updike's depiction of the Hester figure throughout the trilogy suggests that Hester Prynne is not as saintly or heroic as many readers have believed her to be, and that her appearance in Hawthorne's novel would have been a good deal different had Roger Chillingworth or Arthur Dimmesdale been narrating the story.

One final comment upon Esther concerns her name, derived from that of the biblical queen and wife of Ahasuerus. In that most domestic of books, Esther is seen as a courageous and strong-willed woman, unafraid to stand up to her husband. Through her bold appeal to her husband, the king, Esther saves the Jews from certain annihilation. In addition, Esther is the hostess of two feasts for her husband and his grand vizier, Haman. In preparing the dinners, Esther is all along aware that Haman, who is flattered by her efforts, is an enemy who must be destroyed. The situation is paralleled in *Roger's Version*. Esther Lambert coerces her husband into inviting Dale Kohler to two dinners at their home, one a Thanksgiving feast and the other an end-of-the-semester celebration. During each dinner, Esther cooks for and Roger entertains the very person whom they are both trying to exhaust, manipulate, and spiritually annihilate. There is something rather potent and yet sinister in both the biblical Esther and Updike's Esther, as they cook for and pamper the men that they will eventually ruin.

The fourth member of Updike's adulterous quartet is the other Hester Prynne figure in the novel, Verna Ekelof, whose name can function as a pun upon *vernal equinox.* In a novel sensitive to the manner in which light alters perspective, Verna's name suggests that day of the year in March when the sun is directly above the earth's equator. With her instinctual candor, Verna provides full overhead light. She also signals the coming of spring. Though vulgar, bitter, and even violent, Verna possesses a spirit of frankness and adamancy that reawakens the chilly Roger from his dark winter sleep. She is of the real world, whereas Roger exists in the detached intellectual towers of the university. With her "new world slang" set off against the "old world literacy" of Roger, she is Lolita to Roger's Humbert Humbert.[16]

Verna is also Roger's niece, the daughter of his half-sister, Edna,

16. Lorna Sage, "Narrator-Creator Data," 1189.

from Cleveland. Edna is recalled as "this mysterious sweat-smelling powerful playmate and enemy who lived with my father while I didn't" (*RV*, 135). There is a strong resemblance between Edna and Verna, though in Verna Roger senses "a dangerous edge that in my half-sister had been sheathed by middle-class caution" (*RV*, 60). Continually comparing the daughter to the mother, Roger is thrilled at the fact that Verna is of his blood, and the possibility of incest, of coitus with his niece, offers "a superb sudden alteration in my house of narrow possibilities, of breathless darkness" (*RV*, 139). In his relationship with Verna, who is young enough to be his daughter, Roger relives the youthful pains and desires that he once experienced with Verna's mother. In effect, Verna simultaneously plays the roles of Hester and Pearl; Roger was never able to become sexually involved with Edna (a Hester figure of sorts), and so he pulls closer to her through her daughter Verna (a Pearl who becomes a Hester). Once again, Updike demonstrates how human beings interact with other human beings through the agency of a third party.

Roger's first meeting with Verna resembles Chillingworth's initial meeting with Hester in prison. Both Hawthorne's Roger, disguised as a physician, and Updike's Roger, disguised as a thoughtful uncle, appear before the much younger woman in the hopes of acquiring more information about the other man, Dimmesdale/Kohler. Like Hester, Verna finds herself trapped, here in a lower-class "prisonlike project," where she is burdened with a baby that she does not want. Much as Chillingworth heals Pearl by giving her a draught to calm her crying, Roger Lambert takes the "screaming infant [Paula] into my lap" and soothes her (later in the novel he will rescue her from her mother and take her to the hospital). In *The Scarlet Letter* this scene, described as the "interview," closes with Chillingworth stating, "I find here a woman, a man, a child, amongst whom and myself there exist the closest ligaments. No matter whether of love or hate; no matter whether of right or wrong!" (*SL*, 76). Roger Lambert perceives a similar bond with Verna, Dale, and Paula, and in the course of the novel he attempts to manipulate and move through their lives.

One might wonder initially why Roger is drawn to the crude and abusive Verna, yet a variety of reasons, in addition to the fact that Verna is a young woman, present themselves: Verna can give him information about Dale; Verna reminds Roger of Edna and offers the vicarious opportunity for the sexual consummation that he was never able to achieve with his half-sister; Verna offers to Roger, a man fascinated with heresy, the sweet possibility of violation of the taboo of incest; Verna becomes a vehicle through which Roger can compete with Dale; there is a reality to Verna's poverty and lifestyle that Roger finds unfamiliar and attractive; and Verna's resistance and her refusal to be controlled challenge Roger. As Nicholas Spice explains, "the only area of Roger's experience which seems to originate entirely outside his head is occupied by Verna"; she is the willful other, the unstable and resistant woman who nevertheless possesses an instinctual understanding of the needs of this isolated and unhappy man. Though Verna is an unpolished Hester, she nevertheless resembles Hawthorne's heroine, who was, in Updike's words, "tough and defiant and practical."[17] Rejected and shunned by polite society, Verna is the portrait of the contemporary outcast and inner-city scarlet woman. And she forces the reader to reconsider Hester Prynne as less a romantic figure of passion and more a defiant and outcast woman.

If Verna is Hester, then Paula is Pearl. Like Pearl, Paula is a child in search of a father, as reflected in her frequent references to Roger Lambert as "Da?" Lambert, of course, is not the father; he only recently met Verna, and the father is most likely black, as reflected in the child's coffee-colored complexion. As with Pearl, Paula is also an accident, an unplanned baby. Yet Pearl finds in Hester a generous and loving mother. Verna, on the other hand, is irresponsible, selfish, abusive, and immature—the worst of mothers. She names the racially mixed Paula after her own father Paul (to "serve him right" for having kicked her out), and she refers to the child with the most vituperative sobriquets: "the little bitch," "the little cunt," "little Shitface." A victim of anger and hostility, Paula represents the illegitimate child in contemporary America. She is not the precious gift that Hester received, but rather a significant burden with which Verna must deal. Although Hester has a difficult time disciplining Pearl, and though she at one point threatens to "shut thee into the dark closet!," she is a sympathetic and loving presence (*SL*, 181). Or is she? Lawrence contends that Hester's relationship with Pearl has a darker side: "Hester simply

17. Spice, "Underparts," 8; Updike, Letter to the author, January 26, 1989.

hates her child, from one part of herself. And from another, she cherishes her child as her one precious treasure."[18] From Lawrence's perspective Hester is scared of and angry at the result of her sin—Pearl; however, as with so much else in *The Scarlet Letter,* Hawthorne disguises and represses Hester's darker range of feelings toward her daughter. Through his creation of Verna and Paula, Updike once again follows Lawrence's reading, casting the contemporary version of Hester as an impoverished single mother who abuses and resents her unwanted child, Pearl. Updike's updated illustration of the illegitimate American family bears a degree of literary realism not found in Hawthorne.

Paula is also significant because of her mixed racial features.[19] Described by Roger as the "little tawny container of mixed bloods," Paula may not be as controversial a presence as the illegitimate Pearl was in a fictional seventeenth-century America, yet she is just as likely to become victimized as Pearl. As Roger explains, "Her face was destined to be the site of a delicate war between Negroid and Caucasian features" (*RV,* 62). Much as Pearl was the product of blood that was not meant to mix, so is Paula. And though Paula may be a sign of increased integration in America, she is nevertheless victimized by her situation. Her father, who has abandoned her, has nothing of black culture to give to her, and her mother, who views Paula as a reminder that she herself is not normal (to have produced a biracial baby), vents her frustration and abuse on the defenseless child. Paula must rely upon her foster parents, Roger and Esther, who provide generous assistance and prevent the authorities from separating her from her mother (much as Dimmesdale prevents the colony's leadership from taking Pearl from Hester). Not only does their semiadoption of her restore faith in an otherwise unnurturing depiction of America, but it also provides another parallel to *The Scarlet Letter:* Paula, like Pearl, becomes to some extent the beneficiary and heir to Lambert/Chillingworth.

As the novel unravels, Roger's need to follow the steps of Dale and to see the world through Dale's eyes intensifies. One recalls

18. *Studies,* 104.
19. Updike's own grandchildren are of "mixed blood," as he writes in his essay "A Letter to My Grandsons," 164.

how in *The Scarlet Letter* we learn that Dimmesdale "had constantly a dim perception of some evil influence watching over him" (*SL*, 140). Dale Kohler shares this sensation, imagining "an invisible third party" watching his movements. Like Roger Chillingworth and Miles Coverdale before him, Roger Lambert is a voyeur, feeding off of and delighting in the secret observation of others. As with Coverdale, Roger Lambert's "prying curiosity" can be read as a "displacement of his suppressed erotic desire."[20] Unwilling and perhaps unable to indulge in sexual satisfaction with his wife, Roger resorts to peeking at the lives of others as a means to arousal. Much as Thomas Marshfield became stimulated by writing sexually provocative scenes in his diary, Roger Lambert arouses himself by envisioning his wife and her lover engaged in fiercely vigorous sex. And Roger's voyeurism is not limited to imaginative peeking. Occasionally he spies upon his neighbors, the Kriegmans, through his back window, and upon arriving home from work one evening he spies upon his wife through the front window of his house, envisaging her as nourishment for his primitive urges. For Roger there is something scandalous, exhilarating, primal, and empowering about spying upon others.

Lambert's excessive voyeuristic tendencies appear to emanate from his childhood in Cleveland. A voyeur's detachment from the external world, which renders him able to experience reality only from a distance and in fantasy, is often traceable to childhood disturbance.[21] Freud locates the voyeuristic urge in infantile witness of the primal scene. Though Roger provides no evidence that he was witness to such an event, he does adequately outline the early years of his life as a time of abandonment, betrayal, and anxiety. While Roger's mother was pregnant with him, Roger's father was having an affair, and a year later Roger's father left them and remarried, having a daughter with his new wife. Roger's resentment is naturally intense and well distributed. He resents his father for having deserted him and his mother; he resents his stepmother for her "vampishness," which "pre-natally wrecked my life"; and he resents Edna for being able to live with her affluent father. His sense of betrayal is so acute that he describes his stepmother, Ver-

20. Brodhead, *Hawthorne, Melville, and the Novel*, 101.
21. Spice, "Underparts," 8.

onica (whose name, impressed as an image in the mind of Roger, is in line with the focus of the novel, suggesting as it does an image of Christ's face impressed upon a cloth), as having stolen his father "while I was asleep in my mother's womb" (*RV*, 139). Whether or not these events were the cause, Roger's birth was rather painful and violent: "My mother with her narrow pelvis writhed from dark to dark" (*RV*, 190). Prenatally, Roger's life was adversely affected because of the sexual vagaries of those adults on whom he would become dependent. Roger emerged in birth as a victim and outsider, and his lifelong reaction has been to seize control, modulating and manipulating the lives of others. In addition, one cannot help but wonder whether Updike is suggesting that the seeds for Roger Lambert's voyeurism were somehow acquired during his traumatic prenatal months. During that time period, Updike suggests, Roger's mother was no doubt emotionally torn by, and perhaps even projecting her own imaginative pictures of, the sexual infidelities taking place between her husband and Veronica. Perhaps in some mysterious manner, Roger's imaginative pictures of Dale and Esther return him to the safety and comfort of the womb.

As with most voyeurs, Roger Lambert is obsessed with sexuality, and mental-voyeuristic sex appears far more satisfying to him than engaging in the actual physical act: "At a certain age and beyond, the best sex is head sex—sex kept safe in the head" (*RV*, 190). Such an attitude no doubt comes from age and from the fact that a marriage that was once sexually satisfying has become stale; a chemical intensity that once existed between Esther and Roger has been displaced. Roger, however, experiences tremendous pleasure in concocting detailed and explicit pornographic fantasies about his wife and Dale: "She becomes his mistress, a hundred-pound packet of shameless, tender carnality. They strip, they fuck. But first—wait, willing words!—they kiss: together they pry open above the thickness of Esther's chilled clothes a window of warm lips and saliva" (*RV*, 194). In this instance Roger is so exhilarated by his vision of the imminent consummation that rather comically he verbalizes prematurely; he must then rewind his fantasy and begin again. The act of seeing is a creative sexual stimulant for Roger, and once again Updike follows in the steps of Hawthorne and James: "Intimate and erotic passion has the customary status, in James as in Hawthorne, of a pleasure at second hand. The love-ideal of their most typical characters is to get someone else to fall in love, so that they can watch and speculate."[22] Though Roger ultimately consummates his avuncular relationship with Verna, he discovers that his memory of his actual sexual encounter with her "is less distinct in my refractory mind than my flexible wife's many pictured infidelities with Dale" (*RV*, 280).

The only sexual intercourse that Roger actually experiences in the novel is with Verna, and to some degree that transaction is one of prostitution (Roger gives her money each time he leaves). Furthermore, that shared intimacy is pleasurable less because of physical stimulation and more because of what it signifies. In sleeping with Verna, Roger realizes the deferred pleasure of vicariously sleeping with Edna. Moreover, sleeping with Verna presents for the conservative and shielded Roger the challenge of combatting risk and danger: VD, AIDS, incest, embarrassment. Finally, in sleeping with Verna, Roger seeks a negative form of transcendence: "We had no further to fall. Lying there with Verna, gazing upward, I saw how much majesty resides in our continuing to love and honor God even as He inflicts blows upon us—as much as resides in the silence He maintains so that we may enjoy and explore our human freedom. This was *my* proof of His existence. . . . So great a fall proves great heights. Sweet certainty invaded me" (*RV*, 281). As Dale aspires to rise to the heights of God, Roger bids to sink into transcendence. Envisaging himself and Verna as "partners in incest, adultery, and child abuse," Roger basks in the state to which he and his niece have fallen. Utilizing Barthian theology as a justification for his irresponsible behavior, Lambert claims that such behavior leads to a restoration of his faith in God and in God's majesty: "I . . . [committed] deliberate abominations so as to widen and deepen the field in which God's forgiveness can magnificently play" (*RV*, 289). Whether or not we believe Roger, it should be noted that after intercourse with Verna he "felt such cheerful lust for [Esther] as not for years" (*RV*, 284). His feelings for his wife have been stimulated and renewed by intercourse with his niece.

22. Brodhead, *School of Hawthorne*, 188.

What sets *Roger's Version* apart from previous Updike novels is the injection of natural science and computer science. There is a tremendous amount of knowledge and stimuli to digest in the contemporary world, and Updike, who makes the most ambitious of efforts to bring together such a wide assortment of varying strands of knowledge and information, explains the novel as follows:

> The book as a whole, in its novelistic life as an assembly of images, concerns information itself: the intersection of systems of erudition, and the strain of the demands that modern man makes upon his own brain. Pre-scientific hunting man, too, had a busy brain, extensively stocked with plant and animal lore and with memorized mythology— indeed, our utilized memory is surely inferior to his. But he was not oppressed, as are we, by torrents of freshly manufactured input . . . and by our nagging awareness of vast quantities of information, in books, films, tapes, and journals, that we should, ideally, master.[23]

In the course of *Roger's Version*, Roger Lambert is exposed to vast amounts of information outside of his discipline. From Dale Kohler he hears of Boolean math, vector and raster graphics, cosmological and evolutionary theory, and Verna introduces him to the unfamiliar pop sounds of Cyndi Lauper and Madonna. In Roger's house the television, radio, and stereo provide a continual cacophonous transmission of visual and aural stimuli, in which Roger and his family are besieged by *Gilligan's Island*, Pavarotti, and commercials for Preparation H. With such a wide range of stimuli to digest, each character finds himself in the education business, teaching or learning from someone else. Roger learns about pop culture and urban poverty from Verna, and in turn he teaches her about American literature and bourgeois life. At Thanksgiving, Dale teaches Roger, Richie, Esther, and Verna about how computers work, then at Roger's end-of-the-semester party, Dale becomes sacrificial student to Myron Kriegman's lecture on the origin of the universe. Each character assumes an advantage over the others by virtue of what he or she knows; however, in the long run, as Roger relates, "we all know, relatively, less and less, in this world where there is too much to be known, and too little hope of its adding up to anything" (*RV*, 168). Roger is frustrated by the contemporary

---

23. "A 'Special Message,' [*Roger's Version*]," 857.

glut of information that he will never master, the "waste" to which Updike continually refers in the novel, and his only solace is in God, an "eye of Heaven," Who knows all and sees all.

In a novel focused upon our visual ability to perceive and digest information, the computer offers a new way of seeing, a new way of understanding the glut of information that exists in the world. Though Updike remarks in an address at MIT that a computer has none of the "animal confusion—the primordial mud, as it were—of feeling, intention, and common sense," it nevertheless, as Dale Kohler states, works more quickly than a human being and provides a different field of vision: "It's not quite like a photographer sitting down in front of a scene, or even a painter doing what's in front of him dab after dab. In computer graphics, you store the mathematical representation of the object, and then you can call up the image of it from every perspective. . . . And it does it, generally—we're talking vector now—instantly, as far as our eye can tell" (*RV*, 117). Much as Roger's facility for looking through Dale's eyes offers a new way of seeing, similar to "the effect . . . of a tuning adjustment on the UHF channel," the computer itself, via vector and raster graphics, provides a new mode of vision (*RV*, 125). As Updike states, "We have surrounded our consciousness with vastness—vast libraries, vast galaxies, vastly molecular and atomic entities—and in the miniaturized guts of a computer the complication of God's (so to speak) world meets an equivalent complication we have created."[24] As we soon learn, however, in spite of the computer's tremendous potential, for Updike, God remains hidden, removed from detection by human eyes; and the world remains a mystery, where the only solace is in belief in a spiritual world that exists beyond the physical.

Perched in "his Tower of Babel," Dale works at his computer screen, crashing together data, rotating images, varying his perspective in hopes that the eyes of his computer will seize upon a sign from God (and that his effort can duplicate God's creation). Imagining that "something lies behind" the objects on his screen, Dale quickly alters his viewpoint, as he "seeks to trick his unseen opponent by calling for a tilted mirror to be placed behind the

24. Updike, "Computer Heaven," 814; "A 'Special Message' [*Roger's Version*]," 857.

occulting images" (*RV*, 242). Through this process Dale is afforded a back view of his graphics, in which each pixel operates like a "tiny peephole." Resorting to all the computer tricks and knowledge that he has, Dale battles furiously against his invisible opponent, God, hoping for a sign and yet fearful that "It hates [his] seeking It, and will extract vengeance if he finds It" (*RV*, 248). In a brief flicker, "out of the instant ionic shuffle," Dale sees "a mournful face" on the screen, which quickly vanishes. (Updike explains how he once, while shutting off his own computer, encountered "a curious facelike configuration that sparked into sudden being and then slowly faded away"—thus, the seed for his novel.)[25] Though he has failed to capture "one of God's fingerprints," Dale nevertheless feels as if he has taken "a whorl or two." Resuming his visual search, he now hopes that the eye of his computer screen will seize upon "a face whose gaze could be frozen and printed" (*RV*, 246). Failing to discern the face again, he does perceive a hand, and imagines it to be a sign from God addressed to him alone— thus, the parallel to Dimmesdale's observation of the burning red *A* written across the sky. Enraptured by what he has seen, Dale prints out the image. Unfortunately, it is faded, and further attempts at reproducing the commands fail. Ultimately and inevitably, Dale's majestic effort to see the unseeable is unsuccessful, and in the process Dale himself is spiritually, intellectually, and physically devastated. Roger is delighted; maintaining his Barthian position, he is steadfast in his belief that God cannot be known or seen by man, unless God so chooses.

In addition to utilizing the computer as a vehicle for Dale's search for God, Updike metaphorically links the computer to the novel and to the idea of creation itself. *Roger's Version* is largely about creation: God's creation of the world, Dale's creation of a computer program that attempts to mimic God's creation, and Roger's creation (and Updike's creation) of a narrative. As Updike explains, "A novel is, like a computer, a system for the storage, manipulation, and retrieval of information."[26] And as Dale crashes together data and works to create a multitude of angles on the computer, Roger crashes together images, metaphors, and charac-

25. "A 'Special Message' [*Roger's Version*]," 856.
26. Ibid., 858.

ters in his effort to tell a story. Creation is the mystery in *Roger's Version*, and the two main characters attempt to mimic their God by producing their own creations: a narrative for Roger and a computer program for Dale.

Much as *The Scarlet Letter* offers a commentary upon the history and culture of mid-seventeenth-century America, *Roger's Version* offers an amended and updated picture of America, specifically Boston of 1984. Still a haven for immigrants, America is no longer limited to white Anglo-Saxon Protestants from England. Now it is a land of mixed races and ethnic groups, in which Vietnamese, Portuguese, Irish, Italians, and others share in the "adventure." Verna's biracial infant, Paula, represents America's future, and her rescue by the Lamberts suggests that there may indeed be "something grand . . . in the global mixingness, the living anthropology of so many tints of skin jostling here" (*RV*, 53). In terms of government, the administrations of Bellingham and Winthrop have given way to Reagan, who, despite the criticism and cannibalism by academia, is viewed by Roger as the perfect "imitation of that Heavenly Presider whose inactivity has held our loyalty for two millennia" (*RV*, 128). And despite the glut of popular culture, which makes the world so "stylized and untouchable," Roger is optimistic about America and imagines that someday people will "look back upon this present America as a paradise" (*RV*, 291).

Yet, as in *The Scarlet Letter*, there is indeed trouble in paradise. In Hawthorne's novel the initial gnawing of the worm can be located in the prison, an "ugly edifice" with a rusted oaken door that is viewed as "the black flower of civilized society" (*SL*, 48). Standing in vivid contrast to the wild rosebush, the prison represents civilization and the imposition of the human will upon nature. By the time of *Roger's Version* the New World of Boston, Bradford's exalted "City upon a Hill" and the New Eden, has become so civilized that it is now an urban mass of skyscrapers, glass, and cement, which has overtaken the surrounding countryside: "The city went on and on, following the expressway and the shoreline south, sucking village and farmland into its orbit until you could say it ended only where the far suburban edge of the next coastal city began" (*RV*, 317). Boston (although the city is never named as such, its identity is apparent) has expanded like a monster and devoured the natural environment, replacing it with "man-made" edifices and roadways that seem "anesthetized." No longer a new colony, America has become a map of expanding big cities, in which the recognizable landmarks are no longer trees or hills but skyscrapers and bridges. "Man" and "man-made" scenery reign supreme in a large urban setting, and with science and computers acting as replacements for theology, America appears to have lost a good deal of its spirituality.

Operating as a microcosm of contemporary America, the city proves to be so vast and complex that Roger cannot gain a clear perspective on it. Much as he seeks to know Dale Kohler by viewing him from a multiplicity of perspectives, Roger tries to do the same with the city of Boston (Roger functions much like a computer in attempting to see the city from all angles). Reaching further than the eye can see, and continually in the process of simultaneous decay and renewal, the city cannot be fully understood or perceived from one single perspective. For instance, when Roger drives along Sumner Boulevard, "where I had walked a month before, I was struck by the loss of majesty" (RV, 129). The street, stores, and people have been transformed by the alteration in Roger's perspective (he is now driving, not walking) and by the change in light, season, and weather:

> The sky no longer hovered tumultuous with wind-tormented clouds; instead, a fuzzy, yellowish half-rainy wool merged with the blur of the now leafless trees and swallowed the tops of the skyscrapers at the distant center of the city. The stores that at a walker's pace had levelled a certain gritty merchandising spell appeared in the longer, swifter perspective from an auto to be hopeless makeshift tenants of tin-and-tar-garnished boxes scarcely more enduring than the cityscapes I would once fashion . . . out of cereal boxes and egg cartons, Scotch tape and crayons. (RV, 129)

Roger views the city from street level, basement windows, car windows, high-rise academic buildings, and a sixty-story revolving restaurant; and in virtually every location Roger finds himself, he takes a moment to determine the view, discovering how and where this particular perspective relates to the rest of the city. Dale's apartment, Roger observes, "looks not across the river toward the skyscrapers at the heart of the city but back beyond the domes toward . . . the Divinity School" (*RV,* 195). And Verna's apartment has "a view toward the center of the city," where Roger can see "the summit of a skyscraper with its glassed-in observation deck and rotating skyview restauran" (*RV,* 61).

As an acute observer of Boston, Roger most resembles two figures from Hawthorne: Hawthorne himself, who in his *American Notebooks* endeavors to view the city from a variety of angles and perspectives; and Paul Pry, the protagonist from "Sights from a Steeple," who ascends to the top of a church to view the entire city of Boston. As Shaun O'Connell points out, Hawthorne searched "for the most informing and revealing perspectives for viewing Boston, suggesting that the truth of the city resided in some special combination of perceiver and the object perceived." In his *American Notebooks,* Hawthorne explains how he took "an interest in all the nooks and crannies" of Boston and was inclined to search for views of the city from "back windows." Updike, who has written almost exclusively about small-town life, follows Hawthorne's lead and attempts, through Roger Lambert, to update Hawthorne's description of the city of Boston. For both writers Boston is the American city with which they are most familiar, and it serves as a representation of the national character; one can understand America by observing the city. In addition, Updike, like Hawthorne, utilizes irony and juxtaposition in presenting the visual images of the city, and he too finds little hint of Eden in its grids and sidewalks. Yet Updike's Boston is not the dark and somber place that one finds in *The Scarlet Letter.* "Ancient Boston's communal righteousness," as Updike calls it, has dissipated and given way to liberal values and permissiveness in *Roger's Version;* the fear of sin and God's wrath is no longer palpably present.[27] And the city itself, with its citizenry largely anonymous, has become a rather technologically sterile environment, dominated by concrete and glass extending as far as the eye can see.

One might go so far as to conjecture that Updike found in Hawthorne's *American Notebooks* the seed for his characters in *Roger's Version.* While at the National Theater in May of 1850, Hawthorne observed in the next box a quartet of individuals (along with a new

---

27. O'Connell, *Imagining Boston: A Literary Landscape,* 26; Hawthorne, *American Notebooks,* 496; Updike, "Hawthorne's Creed," 76.

baby). As it turned out, Hawthorne was unable to determine the relationships between the individuals, but he noted that there were two men ("one an elderly, gray-headed personage . . . the other a young man") and two young women (one who "was so dark that I rather suspected her to have a tinge of African blood"). Not able to "make out whether either of the men were the father of the child, or what was the nature of the union among them," Hawthorne watched while one of the young women proceeded to breast-feed: "The smaller of the two girls . . . settled the question of maternity, by uncovering her bosom, and presenting it to the child, with so little care of concealment that I saw, and anybody might have seen, the whole breast, and the apex which the infant's little lips compressed." Few scenes are more successful in linking Hawthorne and Updike than Hawthorne's witness of this bare breast (this scene, in which the flesh of a woman is secretly observed, is exactly the kind of scene that recurs in Updike's fiction). And the four characters could very well be prefiguratives of Roger, Dale, Esther, and Verna, the quartet of *Roger's Version*, particularly since Hawthorne closes the scene with an invitation to future speculation: "I should like well to know who they are—of what condition in life—and whether reputable as members of the class to which they belong."[28] One could read *Roger's Version* as Updike's answer to Hawthorne's curiosity; Updike provides lives and a story for the quartet of characters whom Hawthorne first observed at the theater.

In further regard to Hawthorne's attempt to see Boston, one must consider his sketch "Sights from a Steeple," in which Hawthorne's protagonist, Paul Pry, ascends to the top of a church in order to view the city. Here, at the apex and center of Boston, Pry fancies himself as the "watchman" of the town and observes land on three sides of him and water on the fourth. Wishing he could peek into people's homes so as to familiarize himself with their lives (this is precisely what Roger Lambert succeeds in doing), Pry endeavors to lose himself and vicariously experience the lives of others: "The most desirable mode of existence might be that of a spiritualized Paul Pry, hovering invisible round man and woman, witnessing their deeds, searching into their hearts, borrowing

28. *American Notebooks*, 501–4.

brightness from their felicity, and shade from their sorrow, and retaining no emotion peculiar to himself." From his observation point, Pry follows a young man and attempts to imagine what the man is thinking; he then watches the man as he encounters two women. After following a funeral procession, Pry returns to the young man and two women and finds that an older man has taken the women from the younger man (once again Hawthorne's interest in a quartet of two men and two women, with one of the men being older). After a storm, Pry's narrative ends on an optimistic note with a rainbow appearing in the sky, offering the hope and "glory of another world." Thematically the sketch suggests the human desire to ascend, to approach the majesty of God (Updike's initial title for *Roger's Version* was *Majesty*) and also the ultimate insignificance of humanity in relation to Heaven and God.[29]

In *Roger's Version* a similar scene takes place in which Roger Lambert ascends to the highest point in contemporary Boston; however, the perspective is no longer from a church steeple but rather from a skyview restaurant. The church has ceased to be the focal point of the community; it has been replaced by commerce and elegant dining, and the view, of skyscrapers and gas tanks, is drastically different. Sixty stories high, Roger has now ascended to the best view, the grand perspective: the same angle from which he might imagine God viewing. And the city appears transformed: "From on high the river looked much broader—grander, more primeval—than it felt as you nipped across one of the bridges in a car. The university, which loomed so large in my mind and life, almost vanished in the overview . . . of the metropolis" (*RV*, 322).[30] Enhancing and yet complicating his view is the fact that the restaurant revolves, affording Roger a 360-degree view of the enor-

29. Hawthorne, "Sights from a Steeple," *Twice-told Tales*, 192; Updike, "A 'Special Message' [*Roger's Version*]," 857–58.

30. In his updated observation of Boston, Updike apparently borrows Hawthorne's image of the "tree stump" as a way of judging the scale of the city. In his *American Notebooks*, Hawthorne, while on a hill outside the city, views "the stump of a very large elm, recently felled" and remarks, "No house in the city could have reared its roof so high as the roots of that tree" (7–8). In *Roger's Version*, Updike appropriates the image of the tree stump, utilizing it both as a simile and as a yardstick of "progress": "Like outsize tree stumps, the cluster of a larger housing complex stuck up from the denuded hills that marked, on maps, the limits of the city" (*RV*, 317).

mous city and its surroundings. Yet despite the city's vastness—"it was more than the mind could encompass, it overbrimmed the eye"—it was still not enough. Nor was it all that there appeared to be. In other words, Roger finds that the city of men and women—which strives to be so much, which has spread itself so far beyond the gaze of the eye—is still only a part of the physical, phenomenal world. The implication, as in Hawthorne's "Sights from a Steeple," is that there is a spiritual and supernatural world beyond the physical, which cannot clearly be seen by the eye. Despite his expert vision, Roger knows that human optical facilities are tremendously limited, and he is attentive to the fact that people like Dale, who try to see the unseen, who try to focus upon God, shall only find failure.

The city is finally significant in regard to how it economically divides its citizens. Expensive, beautiful, and residential, Roger's neighborhood possesses a "shady narcotic gentility," which instills in others "the notion that there is nowhere better to go" (RV, 31). Verna's neighborhood, on the other hand, is a "prisonlike project" in which houses are abandoned and falling apart; it is the failed paradise of the Kennedy administration, which attempted "to make a yellow-brick Camelot of low-cost housing" (RV, 58). The denizens of one zone, or neighborhood, do not pass unnoticed in another, as subtleties in matters of dress, makeup, voice, and personal bearing differ greatly. In regard to Dale and Verna, Roger imagines them lulled and attracted by the elegance, comfort, and beauty of his upper-middle-class life and neighborhood. In fact, Verna blames Roger for having taken away her happiness by exposing her to his affluent lifestyle. In turn, Roger is attracted by the "secluded squalor" of Verna's apartment. Numbed by the conformity, predictability, and superficiality of his own neighborhood, Roger is inspired by the poverty and random human energy that he finds in Verna's Prospect Avenue project (this is perhaps the "forest" or "wilderness" of Roger's Version). It delights him to be away from his safe, middle-class existence, out "in this strange part of the city, as strange to me and as pregnant with the promise of the unknown as Tientsin or Ouagadougou" (RV, 225).

Largely because of the differences in style of living, social and economic status, and age, the characters in the novel are attracted to and feed off of the lives of one another. As Ann-Janine Morey points out, "*Roger's Version* is about the disappearance of passion," and it becomes the objective of Roger and Esther, through a cannibalism of sorts, to restore passion to their stale lives and marriage. Encountering fierceness and intensity in the lives of the much younger and poorer Dale and Verna, Roger and Esther feed upon that youthful vigor in order to restimulate their own lives. In a social system that rewards the well-to-do, Verna and Dale receive less in their relationship with the Lamberts than the Lamberts receive from them. With echoes of *The Great Gatsby*, Dale, like Nick Carraway, winds up disillusioned by the East. As Verna states, "[Dale] wants to get out of this area and go back home. He says some people can't hack the East and he thinks he's one of them" (*RV*, 315).[31] Like Nick, Dale has been manipulated and corrupted by those who have more power, status, money, and general knowledge of the way society works. Verna is also manipulated by the Lamberts, yet she is a much stronger character than Dale and is better able to fend for herself. In fact, not only does she manage to extract money from Roger, but she also receives free child care and legal support from the Lamberts. In the end though, just as Nick Carraway retreats back to the Midwest from the wicked influence of the East, Dale and Verna are headed back to Ohio.

Dale Kohler's failure, however, is tempered with a degree of success. His retreat to the Midwest is perhaps no more a failure than Dimmesdale's escape into death at the conclusion of *The Scarlet Letter.* Although the conclusion suggests that relative tranquility has been restored in the Lambert household—Roger has subdued Dale, the adulterous affair between Dale and Esther is over, and the "frantic, disreputable Verna" has receded from their lives—Updike follows Hawthorne in leaving his novel open-ended. Echoing Chillingworth's cry, "Thou hast escaped me!" (*SL*, 256), Roger Lambert finds that Dale Kohler too has escaped. For the first time Roger finds himself unable to envision Dale and his wife in coitus: "I could not picture it, quite" (*RV*, 328). Dale is no longer within Roger's visionary grasp, which depresses Roger. Without

---

31. Morey, "Sexual Language," 1036. *The Great Gatsby* is also concerned, at least peripherally, with vision. One of the central images in the novel is that of the eyes of Doctor T. J. Eckleburg, which loom over the valley of ashes with their "persistent stare" like some forgotten God (23–24).

the stimulus of Dale's presence, Roger no longer has a human presence to feed on. By admitting failure and returning to the Midwest, Dale ironically escapes Roger, much as Dimmesdale escapes Chillingworth at the close of *The Scarlet Letter* by ascending the scaffold and confessing.

Yet all is not over. In a novel that traces how human beings interact with one another through the agency of a third party, Roger anticipates that Edna will contact him: "I have sent Verna to her as a message she must answer" (*RV*, 328). And Dale Kohler, living hundreds of miles away, continues to speak to Roger through the body and soul of Esther. As Updike subtly explains in the final paragraphs, Esther is pregnant with Dale's child: "She has been irritable and abstracted these recent days, and eats late at night, and sleeps more than usual. Most strangely, she has stopped watching her weight; I am sure she weighs more now than a hundred pounds" (*RV*, 328). And on this Sunday morning, Esther is going to church, as she puts it, "to annoy" Roger. Esther's charm, according to Roger, had been her "succulent freedom" and lack of religious faith, but Dale has left a spiritual impression upon her, and he has literally left his seed implanted inside of her: "Whatever emotions had washed through her had left an amused glint, a hint or seed" (*RV*, 329). Dale lives on in Esther both spiritually and physically, and there is little Roger can do to alter this. Finally, Esther's declaration that her churchgoing is designed to annoy Roger strengthens the argument that Esther and Roger have used and manipulated Dale in order to feed the needs of their marriage. However, in closing the text, one must recall that all that has been said and seen has come from Roger Lambert, a man who, despite his excellent vision, is prone to fantasy and manipulation.

THREE

S.
Shedding Skins and
Wandering in Desert Places

In Updike's trilogy one becomes increasingly aware that *The Scarlet Letter*, though certainly the central prefigurative text, is not the only Hawthorne text with which Updike engages in dialogue. *S.*, the most comic volume of the trilogy, borrows heavily from and converses with not only *The Scarlet Letter* but also *The Blithedale Romance* and Hawthorne's letters and journal entries. In addition, one should note that Frances FitzGerald's *Cities on a Hill*, which offers an account of the Rajneeshpuram, plays a significant role in *S.*, as do various other texts concerning Eastern philosophy and religion; this of course parallels the situation in *Roger's Version* in which a wide variety of texts concerning particle physics, cosmology, and computer science affect the creation of the narrative. Though it is perhaps most apparent in the Rabbit tetralogy, in which he cuts and pastes contemporary headlines and news stories into his narratives, Updike has become America's preeminent practitioner of intertextuality (his texts are distinctly built upon the work of other texts and engage in dialogue with those texts), and in his *Scarlet Letter* trilogy we observe an increasingly erudite Updike, who has integrated prodigious amounts of reading and research into his multilayered narratives.

Regarding Hawthorne's presence in *S.*, one finds distinct similarities between his residence at Brook Farm and Sarah Worth's stay at the Ashram Arhat. Although *The Blithedale Romance* has long been considered to be Hawthorne's statement upon his residence at Brook Farm, earlier observations and opinions, which had yet to be transformed into fiction, can be found in his letters, primarily to his wife, and in his journal entries. In those letters, written during his seven-month stay at Brook Farm in 1841, Hawthorne discloses his impressions, describes his work assignments, and essentially keeps the outside world posted as to the progress of George Ripley's experimental community:

> Here is thy poor husband in a polar Paradise! I know not how to interpret this aspect of Nature—whether it be of good or evil omen to our enterprise. But I reflect that the Plymouth pilgrims arrived in the midst of storm and stept ashore upon mountain snow-drifts; and nevertheless they prospered, and became a great people—and doubtless it will be the same with us. . . . Dearest, I shall make an excellent husbandman. I feel the original Adam reviving within me. (Hawthorne to Sophia, Oak Hill, April 13, 1841)[1]

In striving to build and participate in a new community, Hawthorne embodies the quintessential American experience of dissent, separation, and heroic struggle in the hope of building a new world. The impulse to shake off the past and reinvent the world has been a primary characteristic of American culture since the landing of the Pilgrims and Puritans, with literary antecedents such as John Winthrop and William Bradford. And Hawthorne, an indefatigable reader of Puritan America, takes it upon himself to join a utopian community not so completely different in spirit from those communities that arrived on America's shores from Europe.

For Hawthorne of course, as for the Pilgrims, the experiment was a failure. The feverish cold that he acquired upon his arrival during a snowstorm should have been heeded as an omen. Over the following months, he became increasingly disappointed with Brook Farm. The weather was bleak and unbearable: "My reminiscences of Brook Farm are like to be the coldest and dreariest imaginable" (Brook Farm, October 21, 1841). His work, shoveling manure, was exhausting and boring: "Even my Custom House experience was not such a thraldom and weariness" (Brook Farm, August 12, 1841). The community was threatened by financial problems: "My hopes are never very sanguine . . . from the im-

---

1. *The Letters, 1813–1843*; all of the quoted passages from the letters are taken from this volume, 526–92. Except where otherwise noted in the text, all letters cited were written to Hawthorne's wife, Sophia.

probability that adequate funds will be raised" (Hawthorne to David Mack, Boston, July 18, 1841). He was unable to write: "I doubt whether I shall succeed in writing . . . while I remain at the farm. I have not the sense of perfect seclusion, which has always been essential to my power of producing anything" (Brook Farm, Sept. 22, 1841). And eventually he abandoned the communal project, having come to the conclusion that the people at Brook Farm were a rather "queer community" (Brook Farm, Sept. 22, 1841).

Updike's *S.* ostensibly arises from and parodies Hawthorne's Brook Farm letters to Sophia. In the epistolary *S.*, Updike's contemporary pilgrim, Sarah Worth, like Hawthorne before her, leaves an unsatisfactory North Shore life and travels to the wilderness in order to participate in an experimental community, here an Arizona ashram. The letters that account for Updike's novel, all penned by Sarah, mirror Hawthorne's letters in that they apprise family and friends of the progress of the community: "They work you like dogs here, at least at first, and there aren't near enough blankets for these cold clear nights, [but] . . . I am absolutely at peace" (*S.*, 31). Both Sarah and Hawthorne write a good deal about their labors at the commune: Sarah hoes artichokes, drives a backhoe, and writes administrative letters for the Arhat; Hawthorne shovels manure and milks cows. And both, interestingly enough, are placed in charge of the financial affairs of their communities: Hawthorne is elected Chairman of the Committee of Finance, and Sarah assumes the role of Temporary Accountant, a position that she will later exploit for her own benefit. Sarah also shares the head cold that both Hawthorne and Miles Coverdale of *The Blithedale Romance* acquire on their journeys to the new community:

> Thy husband was caught by a cold. . . . It has not affected his whole frame, but took entire possession of his head, as being the weakest and most vulnerable part. (Brook Farm, April 28, 1841)

> Thus ended the first evening at Blithedale. I went shivering to my fireless chamber. . . . I had caught a tremendous cold. (*BR*, 37–38)

> That cold I had when I came is still hanging on. I must say there's a lot of minor illness around here, colds and fever and aches and pains. (Sarah to Midge, *S.*, 52)

The cold links Sarah to Hawthorne and Coverdale, demonstrating how the passage from the known world to the experimental community exacts a traumatic physical toll on the human body, not unlike that of death followed by rebirth. As Coverdale explains: "My fit of illness had been an avenue between two existences. . . . The very substance upon my bones . . . was taken off me and flung aside, like any other worn out or unseasonable garment; and, after shivering a little while in my skeleton, I began to be clothed anew. . . . In literal and physical truth, I was quite another man" (*BR*, 61). The fever literally allows the pilgrim to burn off and shed old skin so that new skin may grow. Finally, we are reminded that those who build new communities in the wilderness are exposed to more elemental forces of nature from which civilized society has made major efforts to protect itself.

Of all the similarities between Sarah's residence at the Ashram Arhat and Hawthorne's at Brook Farm, the most substantial is the attitude that each of the pilgrims has adopted toward his or her new community; from the beginning each seems more attached to the world left behind, and in both cases departure from the commune is inevitable and imminent:

> Thou and I must form other plans for ourselves; for I can see few or no signs that Providence purposes to give us a home here. . . . I am becoming more and more convinced, that we must not lean upon the community. What ever is to be done, must be done by thy husband's own individual strength. (Brook Farm, August 22, 1841)

> I don't really think, *entre* just *nous*, the ashram is going to last forever. I think it's too big a step up for the way the world is now. . . . If I sound homesick, maybe I am. I miss the sea and also frankly I could do sometimes with a pop of Jack Daniel's, the way we used to do after yoga. (Sarah to Midge, *S.*, 119–20)

Sarah and Hawthorne are pragmatic pilgrims; neither commits him or herself fully to the new community. Continually talking of departure and making a number of short visits to Boston, Hawthorne has always one foot out of Brook Farm. And Sarah, officiously instructing her husband Charles on how to carefully maintain their yard (as if she will return at any moment), resists giving herself completely to the Ashram Arhat. Through Sarah's skeptical resistance and her ties to the world left behind, Updike parodies

Hawthorne's brief and aborted sojourn to Brook Farm. In addition, he parodies the American quest to separate and rebuild, revealing the self-deception and hypocrisy inherent in such an endeavor.

Perhaps the most surprising and intriguing link between Sarah's and Hawthorne's letters concerns their tone. Initially one might find a scant resemblance between Hawthorne's adoring and fervent letters to his wife and Sarah's bitter, preachy, and domineering letters to her immediate family. Yet there is one letter from Hawthorne to Sophia, concerning Sophia's interest in mesmerism, which distinctly relates to Sarah:

> Most dear wife, I received thy letters and note, last night, and was much gladdened by them; for never has my soul so yearned for thee as now. But, belovedest, my spirit is moved to talk with thee to-day about these magnetic miracles, and to beseech thee to take no part in them. I am unwilling that a power should be exercised on thee. . . . If I possessed such a power over thee, I should not dare to exercise it; nor can I consent to its being exercised by another. . . . I cannot think, without invincible repugnance, of thy holy name being bruited abroad in connection with these magnetic phenomena. Some (horrible thought!) would pronounce my Dove an impostor; the great majority would deem thee crazed. (Brook Farm, October 18, 1841)

Though Hawthorne has no problem in allowing himself to experiment with an altered lifestyle by residing at Brook Farm, he is disturbed and fearful at the thought that Sophia might engage in some experiment of her own, particularly one of "animal magnetism." The liberated Hawthorne, who has left conventional society to participate in George Ripley's commune, stands in direct contrast to the slightly paranoid and possessive Hawthorne.

Sarah is equally anxious that she will lose control of her daughter and that others will seize that control: "Don't you *see* [your father is] doing exactly what my father . . . did—pass you on like a manacled slave to another *man*? . . . European dungeons are deeper, divorces are harder, and you are more securely locked in where [your father] *can get at you.* There is no escaping Daddy once the van Hertzogs sink their claws in" (Sarah to Pearl, *S.*, 205). Much as Hawthorne advises Sophia to avoid the magnetic grasp of Mrs. Park, Sarah counsels her daughter to be wary of the possessive embrace of her father and of her wealthy Dutch fiancé. Both Hawthorne and Sarah, isolated from the world they know best, fear that their loved ones will be lured away from them, and in an effort to combat such an occurrence they become domineering and possessive. In S., Updike appropriates from Hawthorne not only a vehicle and genre for telling his story, namely the epistolary, but also the seeds for a character type: a less-than-committed pilgrim-adventurer who has an obsessive need to possess and control the lives of those residing back in the world left behind. Through his creation of Sarah, Updike utilizes Hawthorne as a guide, paying homage to Hawthorne the artist and letter writer. Yet he parodies Hawthorne the pilgrim for his rather confused and half-hearted quest and for his anxiety over whether his wife will be stolen away from him by another woman.

As a text that arises out of other texts, S. also borrows, in largely a thematic sense, from *The Blithedale Romance*. Bent upon creating a perfect world, the sannyasins of the Ashram Arhat, like the pilgrims of Blithedale, actually create a society that "repeats" and "intensifies" the features of the society they resist.[2] A community based apparently upon antimaterialism, the ashram boasts of its own shopping mall, which sells gadgets, T-shirts, mugs, and tapes. And it employs sophisticated rhetorical strategies to separate pilgrims and patrons from their money so that the Arhat may drive about in limousines and wear diamond rings. For all of their talk of love and the common good, both Blithedale and the Ashram Arhat decline into unhealthy states of mutual distrust, competition, and selfishness. Both novels demonstrate the inevitability of hypocrisy and self-deception in the utopian community. In addition, S. appropriates what Richard Brodhead discovers as an essential characteristic of *The Blithedale Romance*, namely that under the guise of public ideas, politics, and social reform, a "play of passion" and emotional distress is being carried out.[3] Though Hollingsworth, Zenobia, Priscilla, and Coverdale pretend to be striving toward communal reform, their passions and personal needs—Hollingsworth's obsession with prison reform, Zenobia's need for Hollingsworth's requited love—are what truly drive them. Like the Blithedalians, the sannyasins at the Ashram Arhat utilize the act of communal reform as a disguise for more private desires. Though the ashram strives to appear "heavenly and spiritual," the

2. Brodhead, *Hawthorne, Melville, and the Novel*, 99.
3. *School of Hawthorne*, 150.

desire for power, money, and personal revenge is the driving force. Behind the facade of spirituality, the Arhat is bent upon seducing female sannyasins, including Sarah Worth, who claims that her "entire flight [takes] place in an upholding atmosphere of *love*," while it is actually motivated by anger and revenge directed at her husband and at the patriarchal world.

Though *The Blithedale Romance* provides the thematic blueprint for Updike's spiritual community, that of the corrupt and deceptive utopia, the communities themselves are radically different. Updike appropriates a contemporary model on which to base his community from FitzGerald's *Cities on a Hill*, an account of the guru-inspired Rajneeshpuram in Oregon. In terms of its philosophy, organization, and dynamics, the Ashram Arhat is nearly identical to the Rajneeshpuram. Like the Rajneeshpuram, Updike's commune is a miscellany of Buddhism, Hinduism, human potential movement, Zen meditation, encounter group therapy, Tantric sex, yoga, and a variety of California youth religions and psychologies. In addition, Updike actually appropriates for his fictional Arizona ashram specific details from the Oregon ashram: the sannyasins dress in sunset shades of color; they are primarily Westerners; women operate and govern the commune; the guru is driven about in large, expensive automobiles; and the commune fails because of deception, poisoning, electronic bugging, and fraud on the part of its leaders. Finally, the character of Sarah Worth emerges, it would appear, from a real-life sannyasin named Ma Satya Bharti, who, according to FitzGerald's account, was an attractive woman in her early forties who left her New York stockbroker husband, three children, and middle-class life in order to realize "happiness, freedom and continual growth."[4] After she left the ashram, Bharti went on to write two books about her experience there. The verbally eloquent Sarah is of course a writer, and in *S.* she too has written an account of her time spent living on an ashram. In retelling FitzGerald's story about the Rajneeshpuram, Updike has followed Hawthorne's lead as a social chronicler, drawing his fiction out of American cultural history. Yet, in regard to how *S.* pales beside *The Blithedale Romance*, one wonders whether

4. *Cities on a Hill*, 296.

Updike was wise in writing about a community that apparently he, unlike Hawthorne, knew only superficially.[5]

The most crucial text in the dialogue between Hawthorne and Updike's *S.* is, of course, *The Scarlet Letter.* The allusions to Hawthorne's novel are more apparent and plentiful in Hester's version than in the two earlier volumes. Sarah Worth, a literal descendant of the Prynne family, is a contemporary Hester: rebellious, strong willed, tough, energetic, defiant, and practical. And with her "dark hair and rich complexion," Sarah, more than any of the other Hester figures in Updike's trilogy, physically duplicates Hawthorne's heroine, who is described with "dark and abundant hair" and a "richness of complexion." Like her ancestress, Sarah has been stifled, imprisoned, and betrayed by a patriarchal system, and she too is in search of an alternative lifestyle in which she may assume a "freedom of speculation." In the course of each of the novels, Sarah and Hester break with the conventional world and find themselves in new territory and on new ethical ground. Hawthorne's description of Hester roaming in "desert places" and "into regions where other women dared not tread" is taken literally by Updike, who places Sarah in the Arizona desert.

The Chillingworth figure in *S.* is played by Sarah's husband, Charles Worth. Despite the absence of the *Chilling* prefix, Charles possesses "chilly hands" and is by profession a physician. According to Sarah, Charles represents patriarchal repression, which conspires to enslave and manipulate women. The epitome of bourgeois respectability, Charles has betrayed Sarah by engaging in adultery with a succession of nurses (here Charles loosely plays the role of Dimmesdale). Unable to adequately deal with his rejection and betrayal, Sarah, much like a character from Hawthorne, converts her private needs into a public posture. She attempts to exorcise her love for Charles by turning her misery and depression into

---

5. One might counter this argument by contending that in writing *The Scarlet Letter*, Hawthorne was writing about a culture that he knew only superficially (and yet he was successful). However, I would argue that Hawthorne, through his extensive reading and his family history, was extremely well acquainted and intimate with Puritan culture and New England life. Thus, his knowledge of his subject matter in both *The Scarlet Letter* and *The Blithedale Romance*, unlike that of Updike in *S.*, was hardly superficial.

social and spiritual rebellion. Though there is a legitimacy to Sarah's feminist impulses and spiritual desires, much of her rebellion can be viewed as a subterfuge, in which she couches her private revenge in the guise of public reform.

To fill out the triangle, the Dimmesdale figure in the novel is the guru, the Shri Arhat Mindadali, born Art Steinmetz of Watertown, Massachusetts. Sharing Dimmesdale's first name, Steinmetz plays the role of the religious man and "father" figure. Much as Dimmesdale draws Hester and "the virgins of his church" toward him because of his spiritual and physical presence, Steinmetz attracts his share of women, including, most prominently, Sarah. Yet Steinmetz too turns out to be a fraud of sorts, concealing his past identity under a facade of spirituality.

The Hawthorne parallels extend beyond the triangle. Sarah's daughter, Pearl Worth, resembles Hawthorne's Pearl in that she too is a "pearl of great price whose value will never diminish." And much as the original Pearl cannot always be made "amenable to rules," Sarah's Pearl is strong willed and resistant of her mother's controlling hand. Like Pearl Prynne, Pearl Worth goes off to Europe and marries nobility. America, the country in which the mothers of the two Pearls have embroiled themselves in scandal, proves to be no home to these young women, who opt for a return to the Old World, a place of hope, perhaps, in regard to the future of womanhood.

As a retelling of *The Scarlet Letter*, *S.* is charged with puns and playful allusions to Hawthorne's novel. Sarah is continually pushing vitamin A on her mother, for her eyes, skin, and thyroid. Sarah's female lover, Alinga, is addressed as "Dearest A," and together they live in an "A-frame." Instead of displaying a scarlet A on her breast as a sign of her adultery, Sarah conceals a mini tape-recorder in her bra in order to document the actual moment of adultery. In the town of Forrest, a day's drive from Hawthorne, California, Sarah stays at the Babbling Brook Motor Lodge, whose stationery portrays a child dabbling in the brook while dark, ominous trees surround. Sarah and Charles's North Shore home was purchased from "old Mrs. Pyncheon." And finally, in the course of the novel, Sarah encounters characters bearing the names Bellingham, Blithedale, and Hibbens (for Hawthorne's Mistress Hibbins). These puns and allusions reflect Updike's desire to plant secrets within his novels for his more perceptive and vigorous readers, and they answer to his needs as a writer: "I can not imagine being a writer without wanting somehow to play."[6]

Yet in spite of its comic and playful nature, S., as most of the reviewers have failed to notice, challenges and attempts to significantly revise our understanding of *The Scarlet Letter,* particularly the character of Hester Prynne. Certainly the most controversial aspect of S. is Updike's rendering of Hester in the character of Sarah Worth. As a counter to Dimmesdale, whose public persona is one of verbalization, Hawthorne's Hester is marked by her silence, often of an enigmatic nature. Updike alters this condition, providing Hester (Sarah) with a voice in which to tell her untold story. Like so many feminist voices in America that have emerged from imprisonment and confinement in recent years, the voice of Hester Prynne, strong and aggressive, likewise emerges. And when Sarah, operating as the Hester figure, opens her mouth, many readers may be surprised. An often less-than-admirable figure, Sarah pens angry and bitter letters to her relatives, speaks openly of how she has consorted with a variety of male and female lovers, and pilfers funds from the ashram coffers in order to fatten her own surreptitious foreign bank accounts. On a quest for revenge against the world and against the male species in particular, Sarah possesses a voice that can be nasty, defiant, and self-centered, and as more than one critic has stated, "it is difficult . . . to see any real connection between Hester and Sarah Worth, apart from her last name and the fact that she has a daughter called Pearl."[7] Updike has transformed Hester's silence into Sarah's aggressive volubility, and one must determine whether there is sufficient textual grounds for such a transformation.

During the past 140 years, Hester, for many readers, has evolved into a feminist heroine of literature, a sacred sister, a model of dignified defiance. Mark Van Doren refers to her as New England's "most heroic creature," a heroine who is "almost a goddess." More recently, Nina Auerbach has spoken of Hester as "a solitary icon," "a feminist saint, the vehicle for 'a new truth' of empowered and transfigured womanhood." And contemporary reviewers of S.,

6. "One Big Interview," 499.
7. Lurie, "Woman Who Rode Away," 4.

vexed by Updike's version of Hester, have spoken of Hawthorne's heroine in similar fashion. Michiko Kakutani, chastising Updike for his portrayal of women in *The Witches of Eastwick* and *S.*, refers to Chillingworth's wife as "the lovely Hester Prynne." And Alison Lurie, in a review that accuses Updike of having created "a wholly hateful woman" in Sarah Worth, refers to the sainted Hester as "independent, dignified, and passionate."[8] For such readers Hester has become less a literary figure and more a symbol of the strength of womanhood, someone who rivals Joan of Arc and the Virgin Mary. Though Updike's *S.* is the weakest novel of the trilogy (the epistolary mode becomes claustrophobic), his decision not only to parody but also to recast and question the popular literary conception of Hester is much needed and rather courageous.

To persist in reading Hester as an icon appears, from Updike's perspective, to be a mistake. Perhaps the most competent purveyor of literary realism in America today, Updike provides a contemporary and comically realistic Hester, and yet she is one who runs true to the character depicted in Hawthorne's novel. In a letter, Updike states that "I see Hester, in the context of her time, as tough and defiant and practical as she could be." For Updike, Hester is a strong-willed woman, and that is precisely the point: she is a woman, not a symbol. In placing his own imprint upon Hawthorne's material, Updike demystifies and deromanticizes Hester, challenging feminist and other readings that confer sainthood upon her. In asserting a less saintly and more realistic Hester, Updike follows Lawrence, who views Hester as a "gentle devil," desiring to revenge herself upon the male species for all of their oppression and abusiveness.[9] Lawrence and Updike refuse to acknowledge the legitimacy of Hester's sainthood, not because of sexism or misogyny, but rather due to the crafted irony of Hawthorne's text. Though many readers view Hawthorne's heroine as simply the "lovely Hester," Updike is arguing that she is a far more complex, conflicted, self-deceptive, and secretive character.

Evidence from Hawthorne's text suggests that Lawrence's and

8. Van Doren, *Nathaniel Hawthorne*, 151; Auerbach, *Woman and the Demon*, 166, 176; Kakutani, "Updike's Struggle to Portray Women"; Lurie, "Woman Who Rode Away," 4.

9. Updike, Letter to the author, January 26, 1989; Lawrence, *Studies*, 99.

Updike's readings of Hester are viable. Though Sarah may appear less admirable than Hester, it is because Updike allows us direct access to Sarah's private world, whereas Hawthorne only hints at and suggests what is occurring in Hester's mind. Assuming an outward role of social conformity, Hester in her silence conceals much of her private self from the community (and perhaps even from herself), yet there are clues as to what that private self may be:

> She cast away the fragments of a broken chain. The world's law was no law for her mind. . . . She assumed a freedom of speculation, then common enough on the other side of the Atlantic, but which our forefathers, had they known of it, would have held to be a deadlier crime than that stigmatized by the scarlet letter. In her lonesome cottage, by the sea-shore, thoughts visited her, such as dared to enter no other dwelling in New England; shadowy guests, that would have been as perilous as demons to their entertainer, could they have been seen so much as knocking at her door. (*SL*, 164)

Though Hawthorne does not relate explicitly or in detail the nature of Hester's "freedom of speculation," one can conjecture. Forced into a marriage she did not choose and imprisoned within a patriarchal system, Hester has been driven to a "howling wilderness" and forced to endure public shame and humiliation. Though her passion surfaces occasionally in her needlework, her deeper and more visceral emotions go unexposed.

In exposing the "hidden" Hester, in giving a voice to the otherwise silent heroine, Updike must depict in Sarah a character whose thoughts would horrify and outrage a contemporary community. Though Lurie charges that unlike Sarah, "Hester . . . would never have gone off to the seventeenth-century equivalent of the Ashram Arhat," what Lurie fails to see is that that is precisely what Hester does.[10] The Ashram Arhat never achieves the commitment and longevity of the Massachusetts Bay Colony, but it nevertheless offers a new spiritual opportunity for those wishing to rebuild the world. Much like Hester and the other Puritans, Sarah is enticed by a community that is thousands of miles away. And much as contemporary Americans question those who abandon home and family to journey to distant ashrams, the same attitude can be located

---

10. "Woman Who Rode Away," 4.

in non-Puritans who questioned the behavior and stability of those who boarded ships to cross the Atlantic to found a community in a godforsaken wilderness.

Lurie also charges that Hawthorne's Hester would never be as nasty and "shamelessly self-centered" as Sarah is in dealing with her daughter.[11] Lurie points to Sarah's reaction to Pearl's pregnancy: "After wounding me in these various other ways you want to make me into a *grandmother.* . . . With so many of these teenage pregnancies now it's obviously a childish way of punishing the world. Consider me punished" (S., 206–7). Though little textual evidence exists for selfishness or emotional cruelty on the part of Hester, one should recall how Hawthorne's heroine responds to Pearl's questioning of why the minister places his hand over his heart: "'Hold thy tongue, naughty child!' answered her mother, with an asperity that she had never permitted to herself before. 'Do not tease me; else I shall shut thee into the dark closet!'" (SL, 181). In the context of Hawthorne's novel Hester rarely erupts, yet Updike alerts us to the fact that beneath the textual surface she is simmering with anger and hostility.

In addition to offering a major reconsideration of Hester Prynne, S. reexamines the quest for spiritual rebirth in America. Though Sarah claims that she has left Charles "out of love for another" on a quest in which "Love is the goal," her letters are filled with bitter reproaches and anger. For a character who claims to be withdrawing from the world and detaching herself from ambitions and possessions, Sarah remains intimately attached to objects from her past life and to the memory of those objects. Like a comic Shakespearean heroine, Sarah fails to see her own hypocrisy and hidden motives. And the ashram itself follows suit, striving to give a "heavenly and spiritual" appearance while actually being dominated by materialism, envy, jealousy, and greed. Updike is satirizing the spiritual quest in America, pointing to the naïveté and self-deception in such a posture.

The novel begins with Sarah's renunciation of Western culture and patriarchal repression. In her first letter to Charles, written on a flight from Boston to Los Angeles, Sarah writes of how she has become a spiritual pilgrim, bent on joining an Arizona ash-

11. Ibid.

ram. In leaving the civilized world for a new spiritual wilderness, Sarah is a contemporary William Bradford, a latter-day Thoreau; she is the heart and spirit of the American pilgrim who ventures into the wilderness for spiritual renewal. She discards her old name and identity to be reborn as someone new: "I will change my name. I will change my being. The woman you 'knew' and 'possessed' is no more. I am destroying her. . . . I shed you as I would shed a skin" (S., 12). No longer Sarah Worth, "the little tail-wagging housewife puppy," she becomes Kundalini, "the serpent of female energy dormant at the base of the spinal column." And she acquires through yoga a new vocabulary, which offers an alternative means of framing and understanding her relationship to herself, others, and God. In turning to the East, Sarah follows Hester, who "had in her nature a rich, voluptuous, Oriental characteristic," and she fulfills Lawrence's prophecy that this quality, which "lies waiting in American women," will emerge (SL, 83).[12]

Intertwined with the image of shedding a skin and rebirth is the metaphor of emerging from prison. Both *The Scarlet Letter* and S. begin with the heroines' emergence from the iron cells in which they have been held. As Hester literally steps out of the "gloomy" Puritan prison, Sarah steps out of a cultural prison, namely patriarchal and materialistic America. Sarah in fact states that "the material world is a jail," and she refers to Charles as her "prison warder." She is leaving the Puritan prison of vulgarized Protestantism, in which her ancestors have accumulated earthly goods to signify their own election. Sarah Price Worth, whose name resonates with money and value, is breaking free of her culture's attachment to worldly goods by seeking out spiritual nourishment in Buddhism and yoga.

Yet, in the same letter, Sarah clearly expresses that she indeed has not shed her husband, nor has she shed her attachment to worldly goods. Sarah is still intimately connected to her old identity and to her prior life, and for a woman who has recently freed herself from materialism, Sarah inventories their possessions like an accountant and hoards them like a miser: "I rented a big safe-deposit box and put in it the silver teapot with the side-hinged lid and the oblong salver with the big monogrammed P and embossed rim in rope

12. *Studies*, 101.

motif that came from the Prices, and the chest of Adam flatware and . . ." (*S.*, 7). Her continual instructions to her husband, concerning lawn care and domestic cleaning, along with her persistent interest in their family possessions, alerts the reader to her self-deception. The central paradox in Sarah's character, that she can shed that which gives her her very identity, is framed in this first letter, though Sarah is unaware of the paradox.

The major strand of plot in *S.*, as holds true in all three volumes of the trilogy, is the quest for spiritual renewal, yet the primary fuel for Sarah's quest, and Hester's according to Lawrence, is revenge. Hester had once been "glowing with girlish beauty," but Chillingworth "betrayed [her] budding youth into a false and unnatural relation with [his] decay" (*SL*, 58, 75). Forced into a marriage in which she "felt no love, nor feigned any," Hester comes to resent the power and authority of men. Not only was she forced to sacrifice her "young girl's fantasy," but also she was then expected to spend her life with a cold, misshapen scholar in a wilderness thousands of miles across the ocean and away from home. Through his power, money, and male authority, Chillingworth literally was able to acquire Hester as if she were property. A woman of strong will, Hester was instinctively led to defiance and revenge. However, since open rebellion, particularly on the part of a woman, was not tolerated, Hester was forced to subvert and mask her revenge. Though Hester appears to love Dimmesdale, one could also argue that her affair with him masks, even to herself, other motives, such as a refusal to obey the laws of male authority and a desire to wreak havoc among the male-dominated community by bringing about the fall of one of their finest. Hester is a woman who has largely lost belief and trust in male authority, and she bends herself toward revenge for man's failure.

The character of Sarah Worth very much follows from such a reading of Hester. Though her husband is not an old, misshapen scholar, he nevertheless represents the "dark unheeding illegible male authority" that Sarah feels had "been branded into me" (*S.*, 6). Like Chillingworth, Charles Worth is a physician who, according to Sarah, can "heal the world." In Sarah's eyes, Charles has always been godlike and larger than life: "You were my creator, you had put me here, in this rocky grassy sparkling seaside landscape" (*S.*, 10). Having abandoned her studies at Radcliffe to marry young (as

Pearl will later repeat at Yale), Sarah found in Charles a figure of authority and stability, a figure in whom she could place her trust and worship. Yet just as Hester is betrayed by Chillingworth, Sarah is betrayed by Charles Worth. In addition to betraying her in adultery, Charles has been guilty, according to Sarah, of neglect, emotional cruelty, and of inflicting upon her his "antiseptic chill."

As a victim of male oppression and betrayal, Sarah assumes within her family the role of feminist spokeswoman, attempting to pull her mother and daughter together into a sisterhood while warning them as to the dangers of the male species. Sarah is filling the role that Hester assumes in the conclusion of *The Scarlet Letter:* "As Hester Prynne had no selfish ends, nor lived in any measure for her own profit and enjoyment, people . . . besought her counsel, as one who had herself gone through a mighty trouble. Women, more especially, . . . came to Hester's cottage, demanding why they were so wretched, and what the remedy! Hester comforted and counselled them, as best she might" (*SL*, 263). Updike no doubt finds irony in Hawthorne's lines, questioning, through his creation of Sarah Worth, the accuracy of such a noble and selfless Hester.

Regarding her relationship with her daughter, Sarah sees Pearl as a fellow sister of the "frailer sex" who has also been conditioned by "a million years of slavery." Yet Pearl is young, and Sarah views her as the hope and future of women: "How thrilling it has been for me . . . to see you grow, tall and fearless and carrying your femaleness like a battle flag!" (*S.*, 16). Through Pearl, Sarah has the sensation of "seeing myself extended, my womanhood given a second try." Spiritually and physically linked to Pearl, Sarah imagines the two of them as "aspects of the same large person": "I feel you are with me. Part of you, of course, with part of me" (*S.*, 20). Sarah, however, fears that her daughter will sacrifice her life for a man and make the same mistakes she made, and so she attempts to steer Pearl away from the son of the Dutch count: "I just get frantic fearing that Jan won't let you *grow*—that you'll allow him to put a permanent cramp in the ongoing splendid adventure of your womanhood just as your father with the connivance of *my* parents did to me twenty-two years ago" (*S.*, 157–58). Sarah refers to Jan's family as "vulgar and yeasty" brewers who live "off of human drunkenness and forced bacterial labor," and she counsels Pearl as to how men are intimidated by "free women—women standing upright and having ideas and walking up the middle of the sidewalk with unpinned hair bouncing and flowing behind, the way I've always pictured you" (*S.*, 205). Her "lovely little priceless Pearl," though much loved and cared for, becomes for Sarah a vessel through which she can vent her rage and distrust of men.

Sarah's relationship with Pearl bears some resemblance to that of Roger Lambert and Dale Kohler in *Roger's Version*, and even to that of Chillingworth and Dimmesdale in *The Scarlet Letter.* In all of these relationships the elder figure lives vicariously through the younger one, and to varying degrees the elder figure attempts to manipulate that intimacy so as to make the younger one act toward the elder's own private agenda. As Updike himself becomes older, this aspect of vicariousness becomes more visible in his fiction. In addition, since manipulation and the experience of living vicariously are characteristics most often associated with Chillingworth, we discover patterns of distortion (fragmentation, condensation) in *S.* An example of fragmentation occurs when the prefigurative Chillingworth becomes splintered into a number of contemporary characters, including Charles Worth (the primary Chillingworth figure in *S.*) and Sarah. In turn, condensation occurs when more than one prefiguration is related to a single contemporary character. For instance, though Sarah primarily plays the role of Hester, she also possesses manipulative qualities characteristic of Chillingworth, and she is a clever and deceptive speaker (writer) like Dimmesdale. Once again we see how the lines of distinction between the prefigurative Hester, Dimmesdale, and Chillingworth tend to blur in Updike's version, and in regard to the American experiment of self-renewal, we find that Updike's characters often seek this objective in a secondhand manner by living vicariously through the lives of others and manipulating those lives.

Sarah also vents her rage through her mother, blaming her for having connived to detach her from the " 'unsuitable' attachment" to her Jewish college boyfriend, Myron Stern; for persuading her to marry the more suitable Charles Worth; and for having raised her "to be such a proper little Bostonian female prick." Criticizing and advising her mother, who lives in a condominium in Florida, on issues of health, diet, silver maintenance, investments, economics, and men, Sarah finds herself "disgusted" and "alarmed" at her mother's involvement with "this alleged admiral": "I guess it's not in the nature of women to learn. Seduced and ruined by an octogenarian swindler—is that what you want your epitaph to be?" (S., 164). Through the attachments that her mother and Pearl form with men, Sarah exercises her hostility toward Charles. In S., Updike demonstrates not only how emotions are sublimated, but also how Sarah utilizes her mother and daughter to further her own feminist agenda.

S. tells the story not found in *The Scarlet Letter*, the story of Hester's departure from civilization and of her arrival in the wilderness. It tells of the effort of the spiritual pilgrims to build their "City upon a Hill," and of Hester's attraction to the spiritual man Dimmesdale, and of the time leading up to their public scandal. As a retelling of *The Scarlet Letter*, S. begins with Hester's crossing of the Atlantic, paralleled in Sarah's crossing of America by jet. As Hester leaves the old civilized world of Europe for the wilderness of America, Sarah leaves the comfortable shores of New England for the Arizona desert. Both travel in hopes of spiritual and social rebirth, and both are essentially alone. Upon their arrival in the wilderness, both find a lover and spiritual "father" in religious men, yet both are failed by these religious men, just as they are failed by their communities. In the course of the novels, the lives of the female protagonists and their communities become embroiled in scandal, and the women are forced to isolate themselves in lonely cottages by the seashore, with Hester settling in "a small thatched cottage," which "stood on the shore, looking across a basin of the sea at the forest-covered hills, towards the west" (*SL*, 81). That Hester's cottage looks toward the west, and that Sarah migrates to the west, suggests the continual westward migration that has occurred in Europe and America in the last few centuries. It also reminds us that in America the continent itself is still part of the romance, and that in exploring the physical landscape, the pilgrim-adventurer is also exploring herself.

That Sarah has chosen to leave Charles of her own free will compels us to search for a parallel in Hawthorne's novel. In regard to Hester's exodus and migration to the New World, all we are told, and this from a townsperson, is that Chillingworth "was minded to cross over and cast in his lot with us of the Massachusetts. To this purpose, he sent his wife before him, remaining himself to look after some necessary affairs" (*SL*, 62). This explanation has been widely accepted as the reason why Hester has arrived in America earlier than Chillingworth, yet in a novel in which there are so many secrets and in which so much is left in doubt, alternative explanations are possible. Could Hester have come to America of her own free will? Could her solo crossing of the Atlantic have been her idea, her effort, however temporary, to escape Chillingworth? Through the character of Updike's Sarah, we are made to reconsider Hester's early arrival in America. Was it an act of rebellion? Was it her initial effort at breaking away from civilized society? Was it an early sign of her failing marriage with Chillingworth?

Once she has arrived, Sarah, like Hester, finds herself in a newly formed community that is struggling to emerge despite natural threats from the land and climate and political threats from the preexisting surrounding communities. Sarah finds herself morally and literally in a desert place, a place which offers a new perspective on civilization, and a place in which the logic and constructs of civilization no longer appear obvious or necessary. The ashram offers spiritual and intellectual freedom in which, for better or worse, the mind breaks free of its social trappings and opens itself to possibility. Sarah's arrival in the Arizona desert also parallels Thomas Marshfield's arrival at the motel for ministers-gone-astray in Arizona. Though Marshfield is certainly a less willing pilgrim, he and Sarah Worth both go to the American desert in hopes of spiritual illumination. The desert is the topos of enlightenment and redemption, providing a retreat from civilization and a path to the Promised Land. Perhaps the final wilderness available in America, the desert remains the place where Marshfield and Sarah go to shed the trappings and clutter of the material world. The desert is also where Sarah's biblical namesake, the wife of Abraham and the ancestress of Israel, wandered and lived. Like the biblical Sarah, Sarah Worth is a beautiful woman prone to fits of jealousy and contempt. And just as her biblical ancestress is laughed at for thinking of bearing a child at her overly ripe age, Updike's Sarah is laughed at by friends and family for seeking spiritual rebirth at age forty-two. Both women, however, are essentially successful in their attempts at birth, or rebirth, despite social antagonisms. Finally, the biblical Sarah is a precursor for both Hester Prynne and Sarah Worth: as "a mother of nations," she is the original female desert wanderer, and from her "kings of people shall come."[13]

The Arizona desert nourishes a much different type of utopian community from that found in *The Scarlet Letter.* In Hawthorne's Massachusetts Bay Colony the pilgrims walk about in "sad-colored garments and gray, steeple-crowned hats"; in the Ashram Arhat pilgrims dress in "red and orange," "symbolizing the end of mundane concerns." And in contrast to the cemetery and prison that are initially described in Hawthorne's novel, Sarah writes of the ashram disco, the Kali Club, and of the ashram mall, which houses an electronics boutique. Updike is satirizing the pleasure orientation and lightheartedness of the ashram, in direct contrast to the grim and darkened world of the Puritans. Contemporary America, in Updike's opinion, has become "soft" and excessively comfortable; this utopian experiment lacks the conviction, commitment, and intensity of the Puritan movement. It will fail, as is evident to both Sarah and the reader. Yet, despite its problems, the Ashram Arhat, in dialogue with Hawthorne's Puritan community, forces us to rethink the myth of the Puritans and question whether there might not have been more humor, domestic squabbling, and lightheartedness than Hawthorne allows in his "version."

It is to her friend and confidante Midge Hibbens that Sarah relates her most intimate stories about the ashram. Though Sarah views Midge as "my human archivist," Midge eventually betrays her in rather witchlike fashion (in *The Scarlet Letter,* Mistress Hibbins is the witch who tempts Hester toward the devil). It is interesting to note that Sarah does not actually write to Midge, but rather sends her cassette tapes. As is the case in Margaret Atwood's *The Handmaid's Tale* (another novel about a "scarlet woman," which Updike incidentally reviewed just prior to writing S.), the tape replaces the letter as a record of emotions and thoughts; in effect, the epistolary style is in the process of technological evolution.[14] Much as in the novels of Samuel Richardson, the letter itself, or in this case the tape, becomes involved in the action and drama (in *Clarissa,* Lovelace expends much energy in trying to intercept Clarissa's letters). In S. the tape is made furtively (Sarah conceals

13. Gen. 17:16
14. Updike, "Expeditions to Gilead and Seegard."

the recorder in her bra in order to capture the words of the Arhat), and it records actions as they are literally occurring, including coitus between Sarah and the Arhat. In addition, the tape itself becomes an item of value, a document of secrecies and intimacies, which grants power to the person possessing it. In regard to differences between the tape and the letter, the tape reflects the more careless and unedited process of actual speech; though tapes can be erased and manipulated much as letters, in S. they effect a more genuine and spontaneous transmission of thought and emotion, conveying the appearance of a heightened verisimilitude. Finally, the cassette tape as a vehicle for communication wields a degree of power equivalent or superior to that of the printed word: Sarah falls in love with the Arhat "through listening to his tapes and meditating on his photograph"; and it is on a cassette tape, which is eventually locked in a bank vault in Venezuela, that the Arhat's confession of fraudulence is stored. Whereas writing, literally a manuscript found in a dark attic, uncovers the secrets of the past in *The Scarlet Letter,* the cassette-tape records the secrets of the present in S.; along with *The Handmaid's Tale,* S. signals the advance of electronics as a means of recording and preserving our secret lives.

In further regard to writing and language in S., one must at some point confront the thirteen-page glossary of Sanskrit words that serves, in Updike's words, as the "footnote" to the text, and "like any footnote, it . . . should be read through." Most of Updike's reviewers, however, have found that the glossary does "little to give this book weight," and they apparently have not taken Updike's advice to read it through. As one reviewer comments, "This reader didn't pay too close attention to the details since it's a bother having so frequently to consult the nearly 250-word glossary." Reading the glossary provides the same misery and occasional pleasure that one experiences in reading a dictionary. Though there are some gems—"*mahima* the ability, allegedly acquired by an accomplished *yogi*, to swell to such enormous size that one can touch the moon"—the reading is tedious, and one realizes that the novel itself does not generate the interest in the Sanskrit words that Updike no doubt has and would like his readers to have. As far as supporting its inclusion in the novel, however, two arguments can be made. First, in a novel about shedding old skin and starting over, it seems natural for the protagonist to acquire a new vocabulary, which allows her to reframe the world and her system of beliefs (from a feminist perspective it also seems natural for Sarah to acquire a new language, although Sanskrit, like English, remains patriarchal). And second, as Updike explains, the glossary offers a kind of musical accompaniment to the text: "The glossary as I worked on it conspired with me, it seemed, to underline and echo the tangled, tinkling themes of the novel. The glossary became the novel's music, the poetic essence, mechanically extracted, of the preceding narrative."[15]

Though the Arhat is indeed a loose parody of Dimmesdale, there nevertheless exist substantial similarities between the two spiritual fathers. In *The Scarlet Letter*, Dimmesdale is a figure gloated over and worshipped by the admiring public: "They deemed the young clergyman a miracle of holiness. They fancied him the mouthpiece of Heaven's messages of wisdom, and rebuke, and love. In their eyes, the very ground on which he trod was sanctified" (*SL*, 142). By means of his spiritual and physical attractiveness, Dimmesdale wields power, and through his presence and the eloquence of his words, he "conquers" women: "He met the youngest sister of them all. It was a maiden newly won. . . . She was fair and pure as a lily that had bloomed in Paradise. The minister knew well that he was himself enshrined within the stainless sanctity of her heart, which hung its snowy curtains about his image, imparting to religion the warmth of love, and to love a religious purity" (*SL*, 219). Like many of the women in her church, Hester is drawn to the religious man for reasons that transcend the purely religious. The Shri Arhat Mindadali, despite his short, pudgy stature and "substantial nose," exercises a similar attraction over his followers. Sarah describes him as "beautiful . . . So beautiful": "The posters we had don't really do justice to the *glow* he has in person—the aura, I suppose it is—this incredible olive smoothness of his skin . . . and these rich chocolaty eyes there seems no bottom to, just *pools* of knowingness. . . . I see him drive by every day . . . and you wouldn't believe the *peace* he generates, even at thirty miles an hour" (*S.*, 33–34). Like the other sannyasins, Sarah

15. Updike, "Unsolicited Thoughts," 859; Lurie, "Woman Who Rode Away," 4; Lehmann-Haupt, "The Woman Called 'S.'"; Updike, "Unsolicited Thoughts," 859.

has fallen rather comically for the Arhat. Having been drawn to him almost telepathically from a distance of three thousand miles, she becomes increasingly close to him in the course of the novel, viewing him as "a kind of god, at least the closest we're apt to come."

The Arhat is certainly the most intriguing and amusing character in the novel, and he is the latest in a long line of scandalous and fraudulent religious men in American literature, stretching back to such figures as Dimmesdale and Sinclair Lewis's Elmer Gantry. The Arhat is also a product of his own time, resembling the spiritual con-men of the 1980s, from Jim Bakker and Jimmy Swaggart to the Bhagwan Shree Rajneesh. Much as Dimmesdale assumes a public persona very much at odds with his private self, the Arhat has literally created a new identity and public role for himself. Much as James Gatz becomes Jay Gatsby, Art Steinmetz becomes the Shri Arhat Mindadali. Employing that uniquely American mode of thought in which one believes that one can transform oneself into anyone or anything, Art Steinmetz pulls the ultimate coup. The Jewish boy from Watertown, Massachusetts, who studied sales engineering and business administration at Northeastern, goes to India, learns Hindi, Sanskrit, and yoga, and becomes a bona fide Indian guru. He creates a fictitious past for himself in Bombay in which "his father wanted to mutilate him as an infant to make him a more effective beggar," and he begins dressing and speaking like an Indian, ultimately establishing an ashram in the Indian town of Ellora, with himself presiding.

The impetus for Steinmetz's transformation was a childhood sensation of deprivation: "There wasn't any religion around the house. . . . Spiritually I grew up with nothing" (S., 220–21). Having sensed since childhood that he carried within him "a blank little God," Steinmetz bent himself toward realizing greater intimacy with and knowledge of that God. And by transforming himself into an Indian guru, he ended those years of deprivation, becoming the Arhat, which means "the deserving one": "I deserve all I can get, after the lousy upbringing I had" (S., 226).[16] Like

16. In an amusing aside concerning the significance of names, the *New York Times* reported in 1989 that Updike's model for the Arhat, the Bhagwan Shree Rajneesh, was forced to undergo another name change for rather embarrassing reasons: "Bhagwan Shree Rajneesh has changed his name again and his disciples are confused. . . . the Bhagwan part had to go because of the belated discovery

Sarah Worth, Steinmetz is angry at the world, as if it has forced him into an unacceptable mode of behavior and identity, and like Sarah, Steinmetz is attempting to shed his Massachusetts identity and form a new identity based on his own spiritual and physical needs.

The "romance" between Sarah and Steinmetz parallels and creatively fills in the gaps of the relationship between Hester and Dimmesdale. In Updike's version, Sarah comes to the Arhat in hopes of discovering a new "spiritual father." No longer able to rely upon Charles, whom she once viewed as "something of a holy man," Sarah turns to the Arhat as the figure in whom she can place her faith and trust, and she addresses him appropriately as "Master." Sarah is, of course, working against herself and her spiritual quest. Though she is attempting to break free from patriarchal restraints, she immediately turns to another man for guidance (a move on Updike's part that will no doubt anger feminist critics). A zoology textbook that she finds near the end of the novel helps her to articulate this continual paradox:

> The book talks of "the simultaneous eagerness of the female for sexual stimulation and her inherent fear of body contact with any other animal, including a male of her own species." I found that so touching. The story of my life and all our lives really. Scared of our species. It goes on to talk about how lady gray squirrels . . . "feel torn between two powerful instincts: they want to escape and at the same time they want to greet the male." (S., 248)

Despite her efforts, Sarah cannot release herself from this need for a strong male presence in her life; in essence, she cannot resist the impulse to want to "greet the male," as is most evident in her final letter to Charles, in which she recalls how she used to eagerly await his daily arrival home after work.

In all three volumes of Updike's trilogy, the action moves toward the anticipated act of physical consummation between the Dimmesdale and Hester figures, the crucial moment in *The Scarlet Letter* in which private desire conquers public posture and propriety. What Hawthorne omits, Updike surrounds from three sides, emphasizing and attempting to understand its full significance. In *A*

that it meant 'genitals'" (Jane Gross, "With Guru Deported, Disciples Struggle On," A12).

Month of Sundays the act of consummation is the culmination of the novel, the final scene. For Marshfield, the act, "this human contact, this blank-browed thing we do for one another," is a wonderful and mysterious form of mutual worship. Marshfield's joyous attitude toward human sexuality is a direct response to Dimmesdale's self-imposed suffering over the desires of the flesh. In *Roger's Version* the act of consummation is seen from the voyeur's point of view. Roger Lambert experiences vicarious stimulation by imagining his wife and Dale Kohler wrapped in coitus. Like Marshfield, Lambert absolves the flesh, utilizing it as both a means to rejuvenate an otherwise dull life and a manifestation of God's majesty.

In S. the anticipated culmination is delayed by a series of brief affairs, experimental in nature, between Sarah and other sannyasins. Sarah's first lover, a young and "efficient" German named Fritz, is Sarah's group leader and one of the ashram founders. From Fritz, Sarah learns that in coitus the male is to be "motionless inactive spirit" while the female is "active nature"; in other words, as Sarah exclaims, "the woman does all the work!" The relationship with Fritz, however, is brief as she comes to view him as "a Hun" with "a lot of unresolved anger." Sarah's first homosexual experience, with a woman named Alinga (no *linga*, or phallus), follows the affair with Fritz, and it offers her a peace such as she has never felt with any man: "I felt complete, complet*ed*." Through her relationship with Alinga, who is eleven years younger, Sarah vicariously experiences a sexual intimacy with her daughter: "Through her, my dear [Pearl], I often feel drawn closer to you" (S., 90). And though this time with Alinga proves to have been "the happiest of my life . . . the most harmonious," the relationship is ultimately "lacking in fiber." Sarah finds homosexuality lacking in "full seriousness, the seriousness that leads, biologically, to that tremendous bloody ego-splitting death-defying bearing of a child" (S., 167). On a quest that is largely to get away from men, Sarah discovers that women cannot stir her as men can, and that they do not provide for her the "fascination of a challenge."

It is partially through these affairs that Sarah is prepared for inevitable coitus with the Arhat. The Arhat has been teaching Sarah how to awaken her Kundalini, "the female energy in things . . . [which] sleeps coiled at the base of the spine" (S., 75). During their initial sexual encounter, Sarah wears on her chest not the bold scarlet *A* for all to see, but rather a concealed tape recorder, which electronically captures an act that was too private for Hawthorne to even suggest:

> [Unintelligible.] Oh. My God. Goodness me. Now you.
> *No. I do not do. You do again, Kundalini. And again.*
> Really? Isn't that unfair?
> *Unfair to you. . . .*
> If you say so. I keep going?
> *Keep going.*
> Mm. Nn. Oh. Oh yes, yes. God. How do you do it? (*S.*, 185–86)

By offering us a tape of the very act that led to such suffering and tragedy in *The Scarlet Letter,* Updike disarms the act of its damaging moral consequences. Coitus between Hester and Dimmesdale is no longer an act that can only be hinted at and spoken of in whispers; instead, it now evokes laughter. Yet there may indeed be irony here, since Sarah will later deposit the tape in a bank vault for possible blackmail purposes. Though adultery no longer shakes the foundation of American society as it does in *The Scarlet Letter,* the secrets and shared intimacies between two lovers (particularly the Arhat's admission to Sarah of his fraudulent past) continue to be potentially damaging if unveiled before the public eye.

As in *A Month of Sundays* and *Roger's Version,* the scene of consummation in *S.* enacts a union of sex and religion in which man and woman become god and goddess and in which copulation becomes a form of mutual worship. The scene is limned in patriarchal fashion with the Arhat guiding Sarah through lovemaking (one would certainly doubt whether Dimmesdale had the knowledge and skill to successfully shepherd Hester through prolonged and advanced coitus). Updike's version of the Hester-Dimmesdale consummation in *S.* suggests that Hester was drawn to Dimmesdale not so much out of love, but because of the authority and knowledge that she finds to be inherent in his physical and spiritual presence. And her acquiescence in copulating with him can be read as a sign of her desire for knowledge and experience, so as to strengthen her own female authority.

The great revelation of *S.* is Sarah's discovery of the Arhat's true identity. Her reaction is one of hostility; this is hardly the first time she has been deceived by men: "Shams. That's what men are. Liars. Hollow frauds and liars. All of them. *You're* the nothing, not us cunts. *You're* the shunya" (*S.*, 229). This moment marks the climax in Sarah's hostility, which has been growing since she first left Charles. Her bitter criticisms of men have served as a refrain in the novel:

> I wouldn't be a man for anything, they really are *numb*, relatively, wrapped in a uniform or plate armor even when their clothes are off. (*S.*, 85)

> Really, aren't most men just terrible? (*S.*, 98)

> I wonder now if the precious classic therapeutic silence isn't just another version of the Victorian father's silence, his awe-inspiring absence except at dinnertime, with the same disciplinary implications, at least as regards women. (*S.*, 103)

> Men *do* make you feel foolish. (*S.*, 114)

Through joining the ashram Sarah had hopes of a new relationship between men and women, much as Hester speculated that men and women might someday find more equal footing in a new society: "As a first step, the whole system of society is to be torn down, and built up anew. Then, the very nature of the opposite sex, or its long hereditary habit, which has become like nature, is to be essentially modified, before woman can be allowed to assume what seems a fair and suitable position" (*SL*, 165). Though not primarily developed for feminist purposes, the Ashram Arhat nevertheless attempts to redefine the roles of the sexes within the community. The executive committee of the ashram is run mostly by women: "The Arhat has this theory that women are stronger in selflessness than men" (*S.*, 55). Though the Arhat is the central figure at the ashram, the executive committee, otherwise known as the "godmothers," is responsible for all of the important decisions and policies. And many of the women within the ashram assume a superiority over the men by virtue of their *shakti*, or energy: "A not-at-all-uncommon sight is to see a young sannyasin in his violet robes . . . with a gray-haired woman in her fifties. . . .their superior shakti perhaps gives the women here the upper hand that money gives men outside" (*S.*, 88).

Yet, just as in *The Witches of Eastwick*, Updike expresses his belief that when women join together to wield their power, they are no more successful than their male counterparts, and they are perhaps less successful because they entertain greater expectations, imagining that most of their problems stem from the fact that men are in control. At the Ashram Arhat the women are out of control. Durga, the chief executive officer, is impulsive, reckless, and angry. Red-headed and Irish, Durga is a former Dublin artiste turned radical militant who has shunned her restrictive Irish Catholicism for a more free-form Buddhism. She runs the ashram, according to Sarah, through force and oppression: "You've turned this charming dream of a Buddha Field into Gestapo headquarters" (S., 126). And Ma Prapti, a Rumanian who is head of the medical clinic, whom Sarah had "formerly admired, as a kind of Albert Schweitzer or Mother Teresa," turns out to be "rather indiscriminate in her distribution of prescription drugs" (S., 158). Due to Durga's paranoia that "everybody was conspiring to take her power from her," Ma Prapti begins sprinkling Percodan, Valium, and Demerol into the cafeteria's vegetarian curry so as "to keep us all calm and passive." And Sarah turns out to be the most corrupt of the ruling women, pillaging the ashram coffers to fatten her secret bank accounts in Switzerland and the Bahamas. Having felt powerless and slighted by Charles's cagey and secretive attitude toward money matters, Sarah provides for her future and realizes revenge against the world by stealing hundreds of thousands of dollars from the ashram during her tenure as treasurer (a solid financial basis is essential to realizing independence in S.). Though Hester longed for a new society in which men and women could realize a more equal and amicable relationship, the Ashram Arhat fails miserably. To some degree Updike is heeding Hawthorne's words: "Woman cannot take advantage . . . until she herself shall have undergone a still mightier change" (SL, 165).

Though the majority of sannyasins at the ashram are American, the leaders and founders are distinctly European: Durga is Irish Catholic, Ma Prapti is Rumanian, Fritz is West German. And the Arhat himself, though not European, is believed to be Indian. Once again we have a story about foreigners, Europeans for the most part, who travel to America in order to found and foster a new society. America, with its vast open spaces and its lack of history and tradition, is still viewed as a place attractive to experimentation, where dreams can be realized. Unlike the migrating Puritans in the seventeenth century, these Europeans do not find America to be a "howling wilderness" that threatens death through starvation and cold. A much greater threat comes from the INS and FBI, who are continually threatening deportation. Yet for both the seventeenth-century Puritans and the twentieth-century sannyasins, the greatest threat comes from within their own ranks. Internal dissension, paranoia, and an unwillingness to compromise prove to be the undoing of the sannyasins at the Ashram Arhat. According to Sarah, the Europeans at the ashram did not possess the practical and subtle wisdom to make the experiment work: "The Europeans here at the ashram . . . were a fascinating study in how intelligent and attractive people could go through all the correct motions and yet all the time be *missing the point.* They kept trying to make a formal church or a military organization out of it all; the *delicacy* of our American reality keeps escaping them, the way our whole lovely nation is founded on the edge of a dream" (*S.,* 204). Sarah's disaffection for Europeans is of course heightened by the fact that her only daughter has been swept away at a tender age by a family of "square-headed Dutch folk."

Sarah's attitude toward Europe, the home of her ancestors, is conflicted. On the one hand, she imagines a Jamesian manipulation and cynicism behind the savoir faire of Europeans: "Nothing delights them so much as the destruction of a beautiful innocence [i.e. Pearl]" (*S.,* 172). In counseling Pearl against marriage to van Hertzog, she warns that Europeans "are everything Americans left Europe to get away from—materialist, class-obsessed, cruel in their smugness, and smug in their dullness" (*S.,* 171). Europe bears "the leaden weight of age-old sacrosanct male supremacy," and Sarah imagines European males as a kind of "cavepeople who believe that everything comes down to entitlement by birth" (*S.,* 171, 204). Yet Sarah is drawn to Europe, admitting a nostalgic yearning for the Old World as represented by her old boyfriend Myron Stern and his Jewish family: "It was not just you I was infatuated with, it was your family, tucked with all those others in this hilly wooden three-decker part of Boston I had never been to before . . . so full of wallpaper patterns and kinds of plush and fat friendly knobby furniture and embroidered doilies and doodads still savoring of Europe, Europe as a place of actual living life and not just a vague distant source of authenticity and privilege" (S., 242). Because of her own rather correct and neat Protestant up-bringing, Sarah romanticizes the old European middle class and imagines it as "a haven, a blessed relief from the terrible *sparsity* in which I had been raised, the curious correct emptiness of our lives as if half the normal human baggage had been left back in Suffolk, England, in 1630" (S., 244). Sarah's predicament is age-old: she wants to be someone else, she wants a different past. And though she yearns, or at one time yearned, for the Europe of old, she is brutally critical of contemporary Europe and Europeans.

By separating from the trappings of the past, Sarah attempts to renounce her heritage. Her months at the ashram allow her the opportunity to experiment at role-playing. With her female lover Alinga, she plays the role of the male, the "dark and stormy prince," and with the Arhat she becomes the goddess Shakti, making love to the god Shiva. She also assumes a variety of roles in her letters. When writing to Charles she is the wronged wife; when speaking to Midge she is a feminist adventurer; and when writing to the IRS she is a cleverly obstinate tax accountant. The variety of names that Sarah uses to refer to herself attests to her role-playing and her quest to remake herself. In the course of her letters she signs herself as S., Mother, Sally, Sare, Sarah, Sarah P. Worth, Ma Prem Kundalini, K., Sis, Mummy, Tía Sarah, Sarah née Price, Madame Sarah P. Worth, Sarah Price Worth, and #4723–9001–7469–8666 (the number of her Swiss bank account). Sarah also writes and signs letters for others, including the Arhat and Durga, and in writing such letters she takes on their identities. Sarah is of course not the only one at the ashram experimenting with roles. All of the sannyasins have adopted Sanskrit names, and the Arhat himself has transformed himself from Watertown Jew into Indian holy man and guru. In fact, the Arhat has "organically" grown so deeply into his role that he is no longer sure whether he can still speak in his "real voice": "I'm not sure I can still do it. Even my brain now, when it talks to itself, has the Arhat's voice" (S., 219).

Concluding that the Arhat is not ultimately a fraud, Sarah continues her quest by using his self-transformation as a model: "You *have* relocated your life, Master, and that is what I am still seeking to do" (S., 251). One questions Sarah's wisdom, not only in continuing to be guided by a man, but also in being guided by a man who is known primarily for wearing large diamonds and being driven about in limousines. Yet Sarah has been failed (seduced and then disappointed) by two worlds, New England and the ashram, and she has little else to turn to. Disappointed with America, Sarah returns at the end of the novel to the origin of America, an island in the Caribbean, to study and think before continuing her search: "This place, Samana Cay, is where some recent experts, working from the logs, think Columbus *really* landed, not Watling Island sixty miles to the northwest of here" (*S.*, 244–45). Like Hester, who resides in a "small thatched cottage" by the sea, Sarah is finally seen in her own "lonely cottage by the sea," where she "embroiders" her letters, reads, and ponders the future.

Like the Puritans and Pilgrims before her, Sarah has attempted to begin a new life, yet her quest has been plagued by paradoxes, anger, and self-deception. She too fails to become the "destined prophetess" whom Hester imagines for womankind. As much as she strives to shed skins and reinvent herself, she discovers that there is a fixed and constant self: "We shed our skins but something naked and white and amara slithers out and is always the same" (*S.*, 262). And as she lounges on a Caribbean beach thousands of miles from her husband and home in Massachusetts, she cannot help but feel instinctively linked to her life back there, where she once awaited the daily return of Charles: "As I sit reading zoology or cosmology, or just staring into space I catch myself listening for the grinding sound of the garage door sliding up, in obedience to its own inner eye" (*S.*, 264). Sarah reacts in obedience to her own inner eye; it cannot be resisted, even if it opposes her conscious desires. By the novel's conclusion, Sarah accepts that she is governed by "that little unchanging viewpoint or 'I' inside," yet the question becomes, how was that "I" or "eye" created, and can it be altered? After having transformed herself from North Shore housewife to ashram sannyasin, Sarah finds her inner self to be relatively the same. From this perspective the quest has been a failure, and in the process Updike offers a satire upon the American pilgrim, demonstrating how the pilgrim's quest is marked by hypocrisy, self-deception, and fraud.

Yet from another perspective the quest has been a success: Sarah has acted assertively and independently for the first time in her life, and she has opened herself to Eastern spirituality, which offers a new way of framing the world. Loosely following the path of Emerson and Whitman, Sarah takes to a sort of contemporary hybrid transcendentalism, in which she discovers a spiritual relationship with the physical universe: "There is something in *every*-thing, its *is*ness, that is unutterably grand and consoling. I just feel . . . like I'm carved out of one big piece of crystal and exactly fitted into a mold of the same crystal" (*S.*, 42). The American Protestantism of her ancestors can no longer provide spiritual nourishment, and so Sarah turns to the East, which is less interested in morality and ethics and more interested in liberation. In turning to the philosophy, vocabulary, and exercise (yoga) of Eastern thought, Sarah is awakened to her spiritual and physical potential. Updike, who writes of how he himself, while creating *S.*, became "an increasingly enthusiastic disciple of Indian religions," again demonstrates the continuing decay of American religion, but indicates that the future of religion in America may be grounded in Eastern thinking.[17]

Though the novel ends with the image of Sarah on the beach imagining Charles returning home from work, Sarah indicates that her residence there will be temporary. She plans to go to Holland to help Pearl bear her child, and she suggests in a letter to Myron Stern that she is still interested and available. One also wonders what will happen because of her financial improprieties. Will she be imprisoned? Will such dealings render it impossible for her to return to America?

What Sarah fails to learn from Hester and *The Scarlet Letter* is that renunciation is not the way toward salvation. In Hawthorne's novel, "salvation comes through acceptance, attachment to others and reclamation of all those aspects of ourselves we would prefer to relegate to the attic."[18] Sarah attempts to shed and cut her ties to others, and in the process she alienates herself on a tropical island. By striving to strip away all illusion from her life, Sarah is shedding the very essence of what makes life worth living, namely the dreams and illusions that lead to love and human interconnection. Sarah has also fallen into the American trap of becoming all-consumed by the attainment of money and material goods. Just as Thoreau,

17. Updike, "Unsolicited Thoughts," 859.
18. Janet Hobhouse, "The Salvation Letters," 58.

in attempting to free himself of material concerns in *Walden*, became obsessed with penny-pinching and accounting tables, Sarah Price Worth, in her effort to break free from her attachment to worldly goods, plunges herself even more deeply into the world of finances, tax deductions, investments, and secret bank accounts. The acquisition of money becomes a central concern in *S*. Money enables one to be independent and powerful, and it is through their monopoly on money-making that men for so long have been able to maintain power over women. Hester's lack of money and power forces her into a marriage with Chillingworth, a marriage in which she becomes a sort of possession to him. And Sarah's drive for money assists her in her ambition to become independent. Early on in the novel Sarah opens *"my own independent bank account,"* and she appears to associate her acquisition of a new identity with her new financial independence. In order for Sarah to exist on her own, self-sufficient and independent of men, she must have a healthy bank balance. To some degree, the title *S*. signifies not only the obvious—Sarah, sannyasin, seductress, sex, self, serpent (Sarah as Eve), Sanskrit—but also $. In a novel primarily about spirituality, religion, and self-renewal, money plays a surprisingly dominant and persistent role. The quest for a new identity, intimately associated with the dream of America, requires money, as does a "room of one's own."

CONCLUSION

Updike's "Hawthorne Phase"

Though dramatic cultural changes, particularly in regard to sexuality and religion, have significantly altered the American scene since the time when Hawthorne wrote *The Scarlet Letter,* Updike demonstrates that American characters remain self-imprisoned, divided, and anxious, and that many of the same issues and conflicts continue to persist: the presence and significance of adultery in the community; the struggle on the part of women against patriarchal oppression; the conflicts between matter and spirit, individual and community; and the need to shake off the past and reinvent both the world and the self. In each of these three novels—*A Month of Sundays, Roger's Version,* and *S.*—Updike limns characters trapped by both a repressive middle-class Protestantism (handed down from Hawthorne's characters) and by their own unrelenting, unforgiving selves. Stifled, bored, and oppressed by their predictable lives, Updike's characters follow the same spirit of quest that once lured Hawthorne's characters across the Atlantic. Thomas Marshfield, Roger Lambert, and Sarah Worth not only leave their comfortable and familiar middle-class communities—Marshfield and Worth to Arizona, and Lambert to the projects of Boston—but they also attempt to escape the boredom of their own past identities. Much like Hawthorne's characters, Updike's are in need of a transfiguring passionate experience, and for both Hawthorne in *The Scarlet Letter* and Updike in the vast majority of his work, passionate experience begins with adultery. A violation of communal law and a threat to the social structure, adultery accommodates an inner need for rebellion and offers the possibility of a second chance for a new life, which is precisely what Hawthorne's and Updike's characters are seeking.

Though Updike's stories and his concerns parallel those of Hawthorne, there are several significant differences. Updike's America

122

is not nearly so dark and tragic. The grim opening scene of *The Scarlet Letter*, in which a "throng of bearded men, in sad-colored garments and gray, steeple-crowned hats" stands before a "beetle-browed and gloomy" jail, sets the tone for the novel; early communal life in America, as imagined by Hawthorne, is dominated by iron-willed men threatening and menacing the human body and spirit. Updike's America is no longer beleaguered by the gray, iron men of Hawthorne's sensibility. Rather, a different and less threatening beast menaces the land: a benign amiability that lacks vigor and force. America has become fat, inactive, and excessively comfortable; there is no longer any degree of intensity, either spiritual or physical. Released from the restraints of Puritanism, Updike's America is also released from the claims of tragedy. Marshfield, Lambert, and Worth are neither victimized nor tormented in any tragic sense. Instead, their torment is comic and ridiculous: Marshfield spends his month in desert exile playing golf and poker; Lambert struggles with a scientist bent on proving God's existence through computer graphics; and Worth attempts to free herself of men by following the call of a fraudulent guru who drives about in luxurious automobiles. Though both Updike's and Hawthorne's characters are drawn toward passionate behavior as an appropriate response to their environments, their environments are radically distinct: the oppressiveness of Hawthorne's bleak and primitive America gives way to the comedy, parody, and quotidian reality of Updike's middle-class suburban comfort.

Another difference is Updike's reworking of Hawthorne's shadowy romance into detailed realism. Hawthorne's America is an unreal place, marked by primitive forests, ghostly images, and divine messages written across the sky. As Hawthorne states in his preface to *The House of the Seven Gables*, it is acceptable for the romancer to "mingle the Marvellous rather as a slight, delicate, and evanescent flavor" in his work. Locating his fictions in a "neutral territory, somewhere between the real world and fairy-land, where the Actual and the Imaginary may meet," Hawthorne depicts a world not quite real, not quite believably alive, a world that is nearly otherworldly (*SL*, 36). Although Updike has experimented with such worlds in *The Witches of Eastwick* and *The Centaur*, for the most part his is a more realistic, trivial, everyday world. The "despair of the daily" is what attracts Updike, and he insists that "everything can be as interesting as every other thing."[1] Instead of transporting us to another world and time, Updike gives us a data-filled slice of contemporary life, as real and as accurate as he knows how to make it.

In transforming Hawthorne's romance into his own brand of realism, Updike, however, does more than just create realistic characters and settings; he actually offers a freshly conceived response to human behavior in America. In Hawthorne's world of romance, in which there are deep shadows and much left unsaid, retention reigns supreme. Though passion occasionally bursts forth, it is quickly repressed or stifled. Hawthorne's *Scarlet Letter* presents an otherworldly world in which stoicism, control, and repression wage a successful battle against the force of Eros. And Hawthorne himself, though wrestling with his Puritan ancestors, nevertheless demonstrates his disapproval of passion and immorality through the fate that he delivers to his characters. With a clinical frankness and a post-Freudian desire to verbalize, Updike, on the other hand, allows Hawthorne's characters the opportunity that they are denied in *The Scarlet Letter:* to act and speak freely and to deliver directly their own "versions." Barthians for the most part, Updike's characters are less concerned with proper behavior and more concerned with how to maintain their faith in the divine. For Marshfield, Lambert, and Worth, so-called immoral behavior is not a horrible crime. In fact, it is preferable to the stale and boring middle-class routine, which makes living insufferable. Both Hawthorne and Updike question moral authority and demonstrate how a struggle persists in America between individual impulse and social ethics, yet whereas Hawthorne affirms codes of human morality, Updike affirms domestic adventure and irresponsibility for their life-enhancing and faith-providing properties. And Updike, living in a less repressive moment in American history, is a good deal more eager to confront and examine the more ignoble, base, and sordid instincts of human behavior.

Updike's objective in his trilogy is to undo the traditional body-soul division in Hawthorne, in which matter and spirit are in perpetual conflict. Following Tertullian and Barth, Roger Lambert

---

1. "Preface," *The House of the Seven Gables,* 1; Updike, Interview with Howard, "Can a Nice Novelist Finish First?," 74, 76.

argues for the significance of human flesh. Interpreting the soul's life as deriving from that of the body, Lambert links body and soul together as partners both in life and in death. The pleasures of the soul are also those of the body, and neither should bring shame. Much like Lambert, Thomas Marshfield asserts that "we and our bodies are one," and that "we should not heretically . . . castigate the body and its dark promptings" (*MS*, 135). According to Marshfield, America has for too long denied itself physical exhilaration. And in an interview Updike supports this position, stating that sexual events must be given their proper "size" in fiction: "Let's take coitus out of the closet and off the altar and put it on the continuum of human behavior."[2] Updike's purpose in his trilogy is to alter the relationship between body and soul as it exists in *The Scarlet Letter.* Through an acceptance of the body, the American self can rise from its middle-class malaise, recover wholeness, and experience joyous faith in the divine.

What finally are we to make of Updike's trilogy in relationship to his literary career? Although it is still early to judge, one may conjecture. First, the *Scarlet Letter* trilogy can be viewed as an experiment by Updike, part of a new phase in which he departs from some of the conventions of the more traditional and realistic fiction that defines not only his Rabbit tetralogy but also most of his fiction from the 1950s, 1960s, and early 1970s (the major exception, of course, is *The Centaur*). Though his stylistic brilliance places him at the top of writers of American realism, Updike has still been criticized for limning an America that shares too much with those worlds created by O'Hara and Salinger, James and Howells. With *A Month of Sundays*, Updike begins a new phase, which departs from his more traditional and straightforward narratives. In this new phase, which roughly extends from 1975 to 1988 (though it may even extend beyond and into the future, depending upon what Updike creates in the coming years), Updike becomes more interested in alternative modes of storytelling, humor and parody, myth and mythical types, narrative reflexivity and intertextuality, creation and the role of the artist, voyeurism and vicariousness, science and religion. Though in this phase there

2. Updike, Interview with Charles Thomas Samuels, 442.

appear traditional narratives such as *Marry Me* (much of which was written in the 1960s) and *Rabbit Is Rich*, what conspicuously emerges is a more experimental and postmodern Updike, as evident in the three volumes of the *Scarlet Letter* trilogy and in novels like *The Coup* (1979) and the Hawthornesque *The Witches of Eastwick* (1984). Though Hawthorne clearly is not responsible for all, or perhaps even most, of Updike's textual decisions during these years, his influence is nevertheless significant, and much of Updike's development and interest during this period may be traced to Hawthorne. One may even go so far as to refer to these years as Updike's "Hawthorne phase."

One of the most obvious acquisitions from Hawthorne is Updike's interest in vicariousness and voyeurism. Though the adulterous triangular configuration lends itself easily to living life through others and to observing the lives of others, it is not until *The Witches of Eastwick* and *Roger's Version* that these qualities become a central focus in Updike's writing. Brodhead finds the "deepest bond" between Hawthorne and James to be in "their sense of literature's essential vicariousness," and Updike appears to have appropriated this concern, utilizing it as a vehicle for further exploring triangular relationships.[3] In addition, through vicarious experience and voyeurism, Updike's characters are able to bridge the gap between matter and spirit; Roger Lambert becomes physically aroused after having vicariously experienced his wife through Dale Kohler's consciousness.

From Hawthorne, Updike also appears to have expanded his concern with the writer/artist and the process of creation. *The Witches of Eastwick*, which deals with four "artists" of sorts, has strong affinities with such Hawthorne stories as "Drowne's Wooden Image" and "The Artist of the Beautiful." And the three first-person narratives of the *Scarlet Letter* trilogy resemble Hawthorne's novel prefaces and his *Blithedale Romance* in regard to narrative voice and narrative self-consciousness. Though Updike has written about artists and writers in earlier works, such as *The Centaur* and his Bech collections, his concern with the artist takes on a new characteristic in light of his engagement with Hawthorne. Updike turns away from his traditional third-person narrator and attempts in his trilogy new modes of storytelling (the diary in *A Month of Sundays;*

3. *School of Hawthorne*, 183.

a conspicuously unreliable first-person narrative in *Roger's Version;* and the epistolary in S.), which emphasize the role of the writer and the production of his or her narrative. As "writers," Updike's three narrators appear to be the progeny of modernists such as Nabokov and Joyce, yet Hawthorne also figures in. A highly self-conscious stylist himself, Hawthorne possesses in his narrative voice an anxiety and irony that lead Updike to refer to *The Blithedale Romance* as Hawthorne's "most actual [romance], the most nervously alive, in its first-person voice."[4] And that same first-person voice that one finds in *The Blithedale Romance,* and to a lesser degree in "The Custom-House" and Hawthorne's prefaces and letters, operates very much as an antecedent for Updike's own anxious, self-conscious, and nervously alive first-person narratives. Interestingly enough, though *The Scarlet Letter* functions as the primary prefigurative text for Updike's trilogy, *The Blithedale Romance* operates as the greater influence in regard to how Updike's narrators actually sound.

There are other aspects of Updike's recent writing that appear to have surfaced through his engagement with Hawthorne. Certainly Updike's integration of science into *Roger's Version* and his creation of Dale Kohler as a scientist have antecedents not only in Chillingworth but also in Hawthorne's mad scientists (Rappaccini, Aylmer) and in Hawthorne's own dialogue with the pseudo-sciences of his day, such as animal magnetism, mesmerism, and phrenology. And the concern with religion in the trilogy, though nothing new in Updike's work, is given a more central stage in these novels as Updike attempts to demonstrate how American Protestantism has decayed since Puritanism and the fictionalized time of *The Scarlet Letter.* In addition, there is a darkening to Updike's fiction of this period, and it extends to recent texts, such as *Rabbit at Rest,* which many readers have found to be Updike's darkest and most somber novel yet.

Though Hawthorne may not strike one as an experimental novelist (and though his appearance precedes the modernists by nearly a century), his example has allowed Updike to move away slightly from what he calls "plain realism" and begin to write the kind of novel he contends that he most likes to read: "My taste is for crotchety modernist magicians like Joyce and Nabokov and

4. "Hawthorne's Creed," 77.

Calvino."[5] Whether Updike will continue to push away from traditional realism and experiment with other narrative modes remains to be seen; however, his appropriation of Hawthorne has transformed and enriched his work.

A second perspective for understanding Updike's *Scarlet Letter* trilogy is to consider how it allows Updike to link his name to Hawthorne's. Entering company with Melville, James, Howells, Faulkner, and O'Connor, Updike becomes another student in the "School of Hawthorne." As Brodhead observes, Hawthorne gave such "little guidance" to his followers and was so "uncommunicative" as to his works' intentions, that American writers have been free to reconstruct and reinvent him so as to suit their individual needs.[6] In appropriating Hawthorne's story, Updike is afforded the opportunity not only to deal with the same themes, issues, characters, and plot, but also to revise Hawthorne, to recast his nineteenth-century romance in the garb of a contemporary realism bent upon repairing the split between body and soul. In rewriting Hawthorne, Updike aligns himself with a significant American literary past, and he attempts unabashedly to point out that his work can and should be pondered in relation to that of Hawthorne.

The final question for many becomes whether Updike is worthy of Hawthorne's company. If we were to answer this with only the *Scarlet Letter* trilogy in hand, the response most likely would be negative. The same, however, would be true if we were to compare Hawthorne to the great writers of the Greek myths, with only *A Wonder-Book* and *Tanglewood Tales* in hand. With the exception of *Roger's Version*, which I find to be one of the most significant novels in Updike's oeuvre and indeed in American literature in recent years, the novels of Updike's trilogy are not his most compelling narratives. However, all three works, underrated and under-

5. "A 'Special Message' for the Franklin Library's First Edition Society Printing of *Rabbit at Rest* [1990]," 869. While checking the final proof of this study I read the proof of Updike's latest novel, *Memories of the Ford Administration* (1992). Though one could argue that all of Updike's novels are historical in nature, this is his first true historical novel, in which he contrasts the lifestyles of two eras in American history. In addition, the novel includes a scene in which Updike's alter ego, President James Buchanan (then ambassador to London), meets with the American consul in Liverpool, Nathaniel Hawthorne.

6. *School of Hawthorne*, 15–16.

examined as they have been, are indeed among his more complex, clever, and multilayered efforts. One could also say that these three novels, more so than the Rabbit books, lend themselves more easily to second and third readings and become richer in the process. Updike at his best, though, can be seen in his Rabbit tetralogy and in *The Centaur, Roger's Version, The Coup,* and *The Witches of Eastwick.* What we can affirm, however, is that Updike's *Scarlet Letter* trilogy is significant. It reengages and stretches our understanding of Hawthorne's novel, much as did Lawrence's crucial essay; it reveals archetypal patterns in American culture while simultaneously demonstrating how there have been significant and dramatic alterations in regard to sexuality, religion, science, and other aspects of culture since the time of Hawthorne and since the time of the Puritans; it questions the very moral authority inherent in Hawthorne's novel; and it stands as one of the most interesting examples of contemporary intertextuality.

In addition, from his vast body of work—nearly forty volumes— Updike has proven himself a stylist of the first order and an observer par excellence of the American scene. His ability to capture the essence and spirit of the American experience, and to consider such an experience in relationship to the cosmos and the unknown, places him at the top of contemporary American writers. Though Updike lacks Hawthorne's "metaphysical darkness" and understanding of and obsession with isolation, he nevertheless shares with Hawthorne other crucial concerns, themes, and conflicts: a fascination with community and communal experiments; the anxiety and fear of moral damnation; the conflict between body and soul; and the interrelationship between sex and religion. And Updike surpasses Hawthorne in several areas, most notably in his ability to understand the flesh, in all its complexities of desire and function, and in his encyclopedic intelligence, capable of rendering accessible the vastness and intricacy of contemporary life. Though Hawthorne and Updike on occasion share an inability to generate substantial and provocative plot, few writers surpass them in capturing the mood, tension, and conflicts inherent in the American experience. A devoted and tireless reader of his country's history and literature like Hawthorne, Updike has his finger on the pulse of American life and seems to understand and write about America as well as any writer in the twentieth century.

Though only future generations will reveal whether Updike's work is as successful as Hawthorne's in enduring the ravages of time, Updike has certainly expressed his desire, and through his vast body of work earned the right, to be pondered in relationship to America's first great novelist.

APPENDIX

An Interview with John Updike

The following is from a brief interview that I conducted with Mr. Updike through the mail on January 26, 1989.

Schiff: While a majority of your novels are written in the third person (*Of the Farm*, *The Coup*, and portions of *The Centaur* being the exceptions), the three "Hawthorne" novels employ the first person. In addition, these three novels employ a first-person narrative that is unreliable. Is there anything in particular about Hawthorne that drew you to write in the first person, and anything that inspired you to experiment with a more unreliable narrative voice?

Updike: What's unreliable about them? They're as reliable as I can make them. Even Roger's visions of his wife and her lover, which might be taken as a pornographic fantasy, are borne out in the end, essentially, by her pregnancy. I know the phrase "unreliable narrator" is popular critically these days, but I have nothing to do with it. A narrator who's unreliable, why listen to him/her?

Schiff: As Henry James developed and moved through his various phases, you too seem to have passed through an assortment of phases, evolving and ripening as a writer of fiction each time. How has your relationship with Hawthorne over the last fifteen years or so changed you as a writer and as a reader?

Updike: I forget when I first read him, but each time I go back (I reread *The Scarlet Letter* for S.), and do a short story now and then, it is with deepening admiration. He struck the American note, it seems to me, in a most unexpected place and way. And is the only major American novelist until James to write persuasively of male/female relations.

Schiff: That you have chosen to rewrite Hawthorne—and not those writers in whom you have expressed greater interest, such as Proust, Joyce

Nabokov, or Henry Green—is surprising. In fact, in a recent interview you call Hawthorne "not quite" the equal of James and Melville. Why then Hawthorne? And why *The Scarlet Letter*?

Updike: My God, how would one rewrite the modernist masters you mention, and why would one want to, since they have written themselves so well? *The Scarlet Letter* is not merely a piece of fiction, it is a myth by now, and it was an updating of the myth, the triangle as redefined by D.H. Lawrence, that interested me.

Schiff: Did you intend the ending of *A Month of Sundays* to be a therapeutic success, a sort of resurrection for Marshfield, or is it a relapse into that type of behavior that first caused his "stain" and sent him into exile?

Updike: I see it as a success, and a reconfirmation of him in his vocation.

Schiff: Some reviewers have called Sarah Worth a selfish, angry, resentful woman who is not at all like the "independent, dignified, and passionate" Hester. I disagree and find a great many similarities between the two heroines, yet I also see Sarah as less saintly and more materialistic than Hester. How do you read Hester as a character?

Updike: I agree with you. I see Hester, in the context of her time, as tough and defiant and practical as she could be.

SELECTED BIBLIOGRAPHY

PRIMARY SOURCES
Works by Nathaniel Hawthorne

The Centenary Edition of the Works of Nathaniel Hawthorne. William Charvat, Roy Harvey Pearce, Claude M. Simpson, general editors. 20 volumes. Columbus: Ohio State University Press, 1962–1988. Vol. 1, *The Scarlet Letter,* 1962; Vol. 2, *The House of the Seven Gables,* 1965; Vol. 3, *The Blithedale Romance and Fanshawe,* 1971; Vol. 4, *The Marble Faun,* 1968; Vol. 7, *A Wonder-Book and Tanglewood Tales,* 1972; Vol. 8, *The American Notebooks,* 1972; Vol. 9, *Twice-told Tales,* 1974; Vol. 10, *Mosses from an Old Manse,* 1974; Vol. 15, *The Letters, 1813–1843,* 1984.

Works by John Updike
Collections, Novels, and Memoirs

Assorted Prose. New York: Knopf, 1965.
Bech: A Book. New York: Knopf, 1970.
Bech is Back. New York: Knopf, 1982.
The Centaur. New York: Knopf, 1963.
The Coup. New York: Knopf, 1978.
Couples. New York: Knopf, 1968.
Hugging the Shore. New York: Knopf, 1983.
Marry Me. New York: Knopf, 1976.
A Month of Sundays. New York: Knopf, 1975.
Odd Jobs. New York: Knopf, 1991.
Picked-Up Pieces. New York: Knopf, 1975.
Rabbit, Run. New York: Knopf, 1960.
Rabbit at Rest. New York: Knopf, 1990.
Rabbit Is Rich. New York: Knopf, 1981.
Rabbit Redux. New York: Knopf, 1971.
Roger's Version. New York: Knopf, 1986.
S. New York: Knopf, 1988.
Self-Consciousness. New York: Knopf, 1989.
The Witches of Eastwick. New York: Knopf, 1984.

Essays and Short Stories

"Computer Heaven." In *Odd Jobs*, 814–17. New York: Knopf, 1991.

"Emersonianism." In *Odd Jobs*, 148–68. New York: Knopf, 1991.

"Expeditions to Gilead and Seegard." Review of *The Handmaid's Tale*, by Margaret Atwood, and *The Good Apprentice*, by Iris Murdoch. In *Odd Jobs*, 425–36. New York: Knopf, 1991.

"Faith in Search of Understanding." Review of *Anselm: Fides Quaerens Intellectum*, by Karl Barth. In *Assorted Prose*, 273–82. New York: Knopf, 1965.

"Four Sides of One Story." In *The Music School*, 87–100. New York: Knopf, 1966.

"Hawthorne's Creed." In *Hugging the Shore*, 73–80. New York: Knopf, 1983.

"Howells as Anti-Novelist." In *Odd Jobs*, 168–89. New York: Knopf, 1991.

"A Letter to My Grandsons. In *Self-Consciousness*, 164–211. New York: Knopf, 1989.

"Many Bens." In *Odd Jobs*, 240–61. New York: Knopf, 1991.

"Melville's Withdrawal." In *Hugging the Shore*, 80–106. New York: Knopf, 1983.

"More Love in the Western World." Review of *Love Declared*, by Denis de Rougemont. In *Assorted Prose*, 283–300. New York: Knopf, 1965.

"New England Churches." In *Hugging the Shore*, 64–67. New York: Knopf, 1983.

"On Meeting Writers." In *Picked-Up Pieces*, 3–7. New York: Knopf, 1975.

"Religious Notes." In *Picked-Up Pieces*, 123–28. New York: Knopf, 1975.

"A Short and Happy Ride." In *Odd Jobs*, 60–63. New York: Knopf, 1991.

"A 'Special Message' for the Franklin Library's First Edition Society Printing of *Rabbit at Rest* (1990)." In *Odd Jobs*, 869–72. New York: Knopf, 1991.

"A 'Special Message' for the Franklin Library's First Edition Society Printing of *Roger's Version* (1986)." In *Odd Jobs*, 856–58. New York: Knopf, 1991.

"Tillich." Review of *Morality and Beyond*, by Paul Tillich. In *Assorted Prose*, 282–83. New York: Knopf, 1965.

"To the Tram Halt Together." Review of *Karl Barth: His Life from Letters and Autobiographical Texts*, by Eberhard Busch, and *Paul Tillich: His Life and Thought*, by Wilhelm and Marion Pauck. In *Hugging the Shore*, 825–36. New York: Knopf, 1983.

"Unsolicited Thoughts on S. (1988)." In *Odd Jobs*, 858–59. New York: Knopf, 1991.

"Whitman's Egotheism." In *Hugging the Shore*, 106–17. New York: Knopf, 1983.

Interviews and Correspondence

"Can a Nice Novelist Finish First?" Interview with Jane Howard. *Life*, November 4, 1966, 74.

"A Conversation with John Updike." Interview with Richard Burgin. *John Updike Newsletter* 10 and 11 (Spring and Summer 1979): 8–10.

"In *S.*, Updike Tries the Woman's Viewpoint." Interview with Mervyn Rothstein. *New York Times*, March 2, 1988, C21.

Interview with Charles Thomas Samuels. In *Writers at Work/The Paris Review Interviews/Fourth Series*, edited by George Plimpton, 425–54. New York: Penguin, 1976.

Letter to the author, January 26, 1989.

Letter to the author, August 14, 1991.

"One Big Interview." In *Picked-Up Pieces*, 491–519. New York: Knopf, 1975.

"The Origin of the Universe, Time, and John Updike." Interview with Mervyn Rothstein. *New York Times*, November 21, 1985, C28.

"Updike on Hawthorne." Interview with Donald J. Greiner. *Nathaniel Hawthorne Review* 13 (Spring 1987): 1–4.

Secondary Sources

Aldridge, John W. *Time to Murder and Create: The Contemporary Novel in Crisis*. New York: McKay, 1966.

Atwood, Margaret. *The Handmaid's Tale*. Boston: Houghton Mifflin, 1986.

——. "Wondering What It's Like to Be a Woman." Review of *The Witches of Eastwick*, by John Updike. *New York Times Book Review*, May 13, 1984.

Auerbach, Nina. *Woman and the Demon*. Cambridge: Harvard University Press, 1982.

Bakhtin, M. M. *The Dialogic Imagination*. Austin: University of Texas Press, 1981.

Baker, Nicholson. *U and I*. New York: Random House, 1991.

Barth, John. *The End of the Road*. New York: Bantam, 1967.

Barth, Karl. *The Word of God and the Word of Man*. Translated by Douglas Horton. Gloucester, Mass.: Peter Smith, 1978.

Bayer, John G. "Narrative Techniques and the Oral Tradition in *The Scarlet Letter*." *American Literature* 52 (May 1980): 250–63.

Baym, Nina. *The Scarlet Letter: A Reading*. Boston: Twayne, 1986.

————. "Thwarted Nature: Nathaniel Hawthorne as Feminist." In *American Novelists Revisited: Essays in Feminist Criticism*, edited by Fritz Fleischmann, 58–77. Boston: G. K. Hall, 1982.

Bell, Michael Davitt. "Arts of Deception: Hawthorne, 'Romance,' and *The Scarlet Letter*." In *New Essays on "The Scarlet Letter,"* edited by Michael J. Colacurcio, 29–56. Cambridge: Cambridge University Press, 1985.

————. *The Development of American Romance: The Sacrifice of Relation*. Chicago: University of Chicago Press, 1980.

Bercovitch, Sacvan. *The Office of the Scarlet Letter*. Baltimore: Johns Hopkins University Press, 1991.

Bloom, Harold. *The Anxiety of Influence: A Theory of Poetry*. New York: Oxford University Press, 1973.

————, ed. *John Updike*. New York: Chelsea House, 1987.

Brodhead, Richard H. *Hawthorne, Melville, and the Novel*. Chicago: University of Chicago Press, 1976.

————. *The School of Hawthorne*. New York: Oxford University Press, 1986.

Broyard, Anatole. "Letters from the Ashram." Review of *S.*, by John Updike. *New York Times Book Review*, March 13, 1988, 7.

Burchard, Rachael C. *John Updike: Yea Sayings*. Carbondale: Southern Illinois University Press, 1971.

Cameron, Sharon. *The Corporeal Self: Allegories of the Body in Melville and Hawthorne*. Baltimore: Johns Hopkins University Press, 1981.

Campbell, Joseph. *The Hero with a Thousand Faces*. Princeton: Princeton University Press, 1972.

Chase, Richard. *The American Novel and Its Tradition*. New York: Anchor Books, 1957.

————. "Notes on the Study of Myth." In *Myth and Literature*, edited by John B. Vickery, 338–46. Lincoln: University of Nebraska Press, 1966.

Coale, Samuel Chase. *In Hawthorne's Shadow: American Romance from Melville to Mailer*. Lexington: University Press of Kentucky, 1985.

Colacurcio, Michael J. "Footsteps of Anne Hutchinson: The Context of *The Scarlet Letter*." *ELH* 39 (1973): 459–94.

Crews, Frederick. "Mr. Updike's Planet." Review of *Roger's Version*, by John Updike. *New York Review of Books*, December 4, 1986, 7–14.

DeBellis, Jack. "Updike: A Selected Checklist, 1974–1990." *Modern Fiction Studies* 37 (Spring 1991): 129–56.

DeMott, Benjamin. "Mod Masses, Empty Pews." Review of *A Month of Sundays*, by John Updike. *Saturday Review*, March 8, 1975, 20–21.

De Rougemont, Denis. *Love in the Western World*. Translated by Montgomery Belgion. Princeton: Princeton University Press, 1983.

Detweiler, Robert. *John Updike*. Revised. Boston: Twayne, 1984.

DeVries, Peter. *Slouching towards Kalamazoo*. New York: Little, Brown, 1983.

Dinnage, Rosemary. "Lusting for God." Review of *A Month of Sundays*, by John Updike. *Times Literary Supplement*, July 4, 1975, 713.

Donoghue, Denis. "'I Have Preened, I Have Lived.'" Review of *Self-Consciousness*, by John Updike. *New York Times Book Review*, March 5, 1989, 7.

Duvall, John N. "The Pleasure of Textual/Sexual Wrestling: Pornography and Heresy in *Roger's Version*." *Modern Fiction Studies* 37 (Spring 1991): 81–95.

Eder, Richard. "Roger's Version." Review of *Roger's Version*, by John Updike. *Los Angeles Times Book Review*, September 14, 1986, 3.

Edwards, Thomas R. "Busy Minister." Review of *A Month of Sundays*, by John Updike. *New York Review of Books*, April 3, 1975, 18.

Eliot, T. S. "*Ulysses*, Order, and Myth." In *Selected Prose of T. S. Eliot*, edited by Frank Kermode, 175–78. New York: Harcourt Brace Jovanovich, 1975.

Elliot, Emory. "From Father to Son: The Evolution of Typology in Puritan New England." In *Literary Uses of Typology: From the late Middle Ages to the Present*, edited by Earl Miner, 345–69. Princeton: Princeton University Press, 1977.

Fiedler, Leslie. *Love and Death in the American Novel*. New York: Criterion Books, 1960.

Fitzgerald, F. Scott. *The Great Gatsby*. New York: Charles Scribner's Sons, 1980.

FitzGerald, Frances. *Cities on a Hill*. New York: Simon & Schuster, 1986.

Gilman, Richard. "The Witches of Updike." Review of *S.*, by John Updike. *New Republic*, June 20, 1988, 39–41.

Gould, Eric. *Mythical Intentions in Modern Literature*. Princeton: Princeton University Press, 1981.

Greiner, Donald J. *Adultery in the American Novel: Updike, James, and Hawthorne*. Columbia: University of South Carolina Press, 1985.

———. "Body and Soul: John Updike and *The Scarlet Letter*." *Journal of Modern Literature* 15 (Spring 1989): 475–95.

———. *John Updike's Novels*. Athens: Ohio University Press, 1984.

———. *The Other John Updike: Poems, Short Stories, Prose, Play*. Athens: Ohio University Press, 1981.

Gross, Jane. "With Guru Deported, Disciples Struggle On." *New York Times*, January 25, 1989, A12.

Hamilton, Alice, and Kenneth Hamilton. *The Elements of John Updike.* Grand Rapids, Mich.: William B. Eerdmans, 1970.

Hendin, Josephine. *Vulnerable People.* New York: Oxford University Press, 1978.

Hobhouse, Janet. "The Salvation Letters." Review of *S.*, by John Updike. *Newsweek*, March 14, 1988, 58.

Hunt, George W., S.J. *John Updike and the Three Great Secret Things: Sex, Religion, and Art.* Grand Rapids, Mich.: William B. Eerdmans, 1980.

James, Henry. *Hawthorne.* New York: Harper and Brothers, 1879.

Kakutani, Michiko. Review of *Roger's Version*, by John Updike. *New York Times*, August 27, 1986, C27.

———. "Updike's Struggle to Portray Women." *New York Times*, May 5, 1988, C29.

Karl, Frederick. *American Fictions, 1940–1980.* New York: Harper & Row, 1983.

Lanchester, John. "Be a Lamp unto Yourself." Review of *S.*, by John Updike. *London Review of Books*, May 5, 1988, 20–21.

Larson, Charles R. *Arthur Dimmesdale.* New York: A & W, 1983.

Lawrence, D. H. *Fantasia of the Unconscious.* New York: Penguin, 1977.

———. *Studies in Classic American Literature.* New York: Penguin, 1977.

Leckie, Barbara. "'The Adulterous Society': John Updike's *Marry Me.*" *Modern Fiction Studies* 37 (Spring 1991): 61–79.

Lehmann-Haupt, Christopher. "In John Updike's Latest, The Woman Called *S.*" *New York Times*, March 7, 1988, C16.

Lodge, David. "Chasing after God and Sex." Review of *Roger's Version*, by John Updike. *New York Times Book Review*, August 31, 1986.

———. "Post-Pill Paradise Lost: John Updike's *Couples.*" In *John Updike*, edited by Harold Bloom, 29–36. New York: Chelsea House, 1987.

Lurie, Alison. "The Woman Who Rode Away." Review of *Trust Me* and *S.*, by John Updike. *New York Review of Books*, May 12, 1988, 3–4.

Macnaughton, William R., ed. *Critical Essays on John Updike.* Boston: G. K. Hall, 1982.

McPherson, Hugo. *Hawthorne as Myth-Maker.* Toronto: University of Toronto Press, 1969.

Male, Roy R. *Hawthorne's Tragic Vision.* Austin: University of Texas Press, 1957.

Mano, D. Keith. "Doughy Middleness." In *Critical Essays on John Updike*, edited by William R. Macnaughton, 74–76. Boston: G. K. Hall, 1982.

Markle, Joyce B. *Fighters and Lovers: Theme in the Novels of John Updike*. New York: New York University Press, 1973.

Matthews, John T. "Intertextuality and Originality: Hawthorne, Faulkner, Updike." In *Intertextuality in Faulkner*, edited by Michel Gresset and Noel Polk, 144–57. Jackson: University Press of Mississippi, 1985.

————. "The Word as Scandal: Updike's *A Month of Sundays*." *Arizona Quarterly* 39 (1983): 351–80.

Mellow, James. *Nathaniel Hawthorne in His Times*. Boston: Houghton Mifflin, 1980.

Miller, Edwin Haviland. *Salem is My Dwelling Place: A Life of Nathaniel Hawthorne*. Iowa City: University of Iowa Press, 1991.

Miner, Earl, ed. *Literary Uses of Typology: From the Late Middle Ages to the Present*. Princeton: Princeton University Press, 1977.

Modern Fiction Studies 20 (Spring 1974). "John Updike Special Issue," consisting of articles on Updike, reviews of Updike criticism, and a checklist of Updike criticism.

Modern Fiction Studies 37 (Spring 1991). "John Updike Special Issue," consisting of articles and an extensive checklist of Updike criticism.

Morey, Ann-Janine. "Updike's Sexual Language for God." Review of *Roger's Version*, by John Updike. *Christian Century*, November 19, 1986, 1036–37.

Nabokov, Vladimir. *Lolita*. New York: G. P. Putnam's Sons, 1955.

Neary, John. *Something and Nothingness: The Fiction of John Updike and John Fowles*. Carbondale: Southern Illinois University Press, 1992.

Newman, Judie. *John Updike*. New York: St. Martin's, 1988.

"Notes from the Editors." Pamphlet insert to Franklin Library edition of *Rabbit, Run*. Franklin Center, Pennsylvania: Franklin Library, 1977.

Oates, Joyce Carol. "Updike's American Comedies." *Modern Fiction Studies* 21 (Fall 1975): 459–72.

O'Connell, Shaun. *Imagining Boston: A Literary Landscape*. Boston: Beacon Press, 1990.

Podhoretz, Norman. *Doings and Undoings*. New York: Noonday, 1964.

Pritchard, William H., and George Hunsinger. "Updike's Version." *New York Review of Books*, February 12, 1987, 41.

Ra'ad, Basem L. "Updike's New Versions of Myth in America." *Modern Fiction Studies* 37 (Spring 1991): 25–33.

Righter, William. *Myth and Literature*. London: Routledge and Kegan Paul, 1975.

Roth, Philip. *Portnoy's Complaint*. New York: Random House, 1969.

Rupp, Richard H. "John Updike: Style in Search of a Center." In *John Updike*, edited by Harold Bloom. New York: Chelsea House, 1987.

Sage, Lorna. "Narrator-Creator Data." Review of *Roger's Version*, by John Updike. *Times Literary Supplement*, October 24, 1986, 1189.

Schiff, James A. "Updike's *Roger's Version:* Re-Visualizing *The Scarlet Letter. South Atlantic Review* 57.4 (November 1992).

————. "Updike's *Scarlet Letter* Trilogy: Recasting an American Myth." *Studies in American Fiction* 20.1 (Spring 1992): 17–31.

Schopen, Bernard A. "Faith, Morality, and the Novels of John Updike." *Twentieth-Century Literature* 24 (1978): 523–35.

Spice, Nicholas. "Underparts." Review of *Roger's Version*, by John Updike. *London Review of Books*, November 6, 1986, 8–9.

Stade, George. "The Resurrection of Reverend Marshfield." Review of *A Month of Sundays*, by John Updike. *New York Times Book Review*, February 23, 1975, 4.

Steiner, George. "Scarlet Letters." Review of *A Month of Sundays*, by John Updike. *New Yorker*, March 10, 1975, 116–18.

Strandberg, Victor. "John Updike and the Changing of the Gods." *Mosaic* 12 (1978): 157–75.

Swigg, Richard. *Lawrence, Hardy, and American Literature*. London: Oxford University Press, 1972.

Tallent, Elizabeth. *Married Men and Magic Tricks: John Updike's Erotic Heroes*. Berkeley: Creative Arts, 1982.

Tanner, Tony. *Adultery in the Novel: Contract and Transgression*. Baltimore: Johns Hopkins University Press, 1979.

Taylor, Larry E. *Pastoral and Anti-Pastoral Patterns in John Updike's Fiction*. Carbondale: Southern Illinois University Press, 1971.

Thorburn, David, and Howard Eiland, eds. *John Updike: A Collection of Critical Essays*. Englewood Cliffs, N.J.: Prentice-Hall, 1979.

Tillich, Paul. *Morality and Beyond*. New York: Harper & Row, 1963.

Trefil, James S. *From Atoms to Quarks*. New York: Charles Scribner's Sons, 1980.

————. *The Moment of Creation*. New York: Macmillan, 1983.

Turner, Arlin. *Nathaniel Hawthorne: A Biography*. New York: Oxford University Press, 1980.

Uphaus, Suzanne Henning. *John Updike*. New York: Frederick Ungar, 1980.

Van Doren, Mark. *Nathaniel Hawthorne*. New York: William Sloane, 1947.

Vargo, Edward P. *Rainstorms and Fire: Ritual in the Novels of John Updike*. Port Washington, N.Y.: Kennikat, 1973.

Verduin, Kathleen. "Fatherly Presences: John Updike's Place in a

Protestant Tradition." In *Critical Essays on John Updike*, edited by William R. Macnaughton, 254–68. Boston: G. K. Hall, 1982.

Vickery, John B. *Myths and Texts: Strategies of Incorporation and Displacement*. Baton Rouge: Louisiana State University Press, 1983.

———, ed. *Myth and Literature*. Lincoln: University of Nebraska Press, 1966.

Waller, Gary. "Stylus Dei or the Open-Endedness of Debate? Success and Failure in *A Month of Sundays*." In *Critical Essays on John Updike*, edited by William R. Macnaughton, 269–80. Boston: G. K. Hall, 1982.

White, John J. *Mythology in the Modern Novel*. Princeton: Princeton University Press, 1971.

Wilson III, Raymond. "*Roger's Version*: Updike's Negative-Solid Model of *The Scarlet Letter.*" *Modern Fiction Studies* 35 (1989): 241–50.

Young, Philip. *Hawthorne's Secret: An Un-Told Tale*. Boston: David R. Godine, 1984.

Ziegler, Heidi. "Love's Labours Won: The Erotics of Contemporary Parody." In *Intertextuality and Contemporary American Fiction*, edited by Patrick O'Donnell and Robert Con Davis, 58–71. Baltimore: Johns Hopkins University Press, 1989.

Ziolkowski, Theodore. "Some Features of Religious Formalism in Twentieth-Century Literature." In *Literary Uses of Typology: From the Late Middle Ages to the Present*, edited by Earl Miner, 345–69. Princeton: Princeton University Press, 1977.

INDEX